7.50

The Fanatic's Ecstatic
Aromatic Guide to
ONIONS,
GARLIC,
SHALLOTS
and *LEEKS*

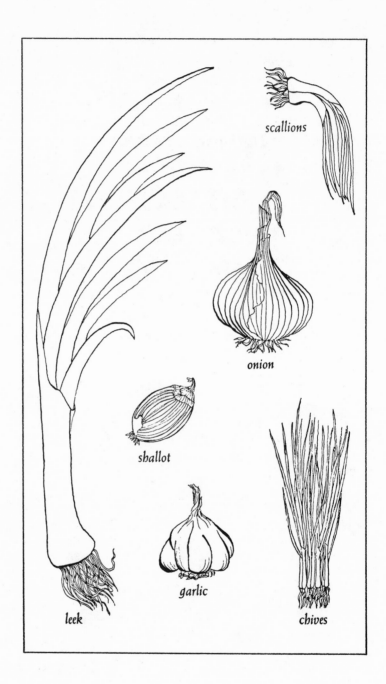

scallions

onion

shallot

garlic

leek

chives

The Fanatic's Ecstatic Aromatic Guide to

ONIONS, GARLIC, SHALLOTS and LEEKS

by Marilyn Singer
illustrations by Marian Parry

Prentice-Hall, Inc. • Englewood Cliffs, New Jersey

Prentice-Hall International, Inc., London
Prentice-Hall of Australia, Pty. Ltd., North Sydney
Prentice-Hall of Canada, Ltd., Toronto
Prentice-Hall of India Private Ltd., New Delhi
Prentice-Hall of Japan, Inc., Tokyo
Prentice-Hall of Southeast Asia Pte. Ltd., Singapore
Whitehall Books Limited, Wellington, New Zealand

10   9   8   7   6   5   4   3   2   1

Library of Congress Cataloging in Publication Data
Singer, Marilyn.   The fanatic's ecstatic aromatic guide to onions, garlic, shallots, and leeks.
Bibliography: p.   Includes index.
Summary: Discusses the history, botanical background, and legendary and medicinal properties of onions, garlic, shallots, chives, leeks, and other members of the allium family.
1. Allium–Juvenile literature. [1. Allium. 2. Onions. 3. Garlic] I. Parry, Marian. II. Title.
QK495.L72S56   584'.25   80-18883   ISBN 0-13-302901-8

HELPFUL FOLKS

*The Author wishes to thank the following
for their tremendous help:*

Marie Giasi and the Brooklyn Botanic Garden Library Staff · Tom
Delendick, Nancy Shopis and the BBG Instruction Department · Michael
Ramirez, Arvid (Slim) Zumwalt and the BBG Gardening Staff · Gerry
McKiernan and the New York Botanical Garden Library Staff · The Staff
of the Brooklyn Public Library, Grand Army Plaza · Steve Aronson, my
favorite cook · Al Balestra · Erica Bernich · Les Blank · Susan Dallas · Sari
Dienes · John Duguid · Dr. Eugene Cruz-Uribe, of the Metropolitan
Museum of Art · Anne F. Harris · John (Lloyd) Harris · Sheena Matthews ·
Sherry Mestel · Dave and Mary Flynn Ottiger, my other favorite cooks ·
Jack Passalaqua · Dr. Sam Ristich · Howard Roberts · Carolee Schneemann
· Shirley Singer, my mother · Dr. Barbara Zeller ·
And especially Pat Lowe, without whom this book would never have been
conceived.

To All the Lovers of All the Stinking Roses

Contents

A QUIZ:

1. What was the first great onion joke?

2. Who wouldn't move his army into battle without a load of onions and why?

3. For what do Romany gypsies use chives?

4. How can garlic help you get rid of a nasty toothache?

5. How can you use onions to get the person you like to like you back?

6. What does Satan have to do with garlic and onions?

7. Who said, "To leek or not to leek, that is not the question"?

8. For what day of the year is the leek a birthday plant?

9. How do you get rid of a vampire via garlic?

10. Why do garlic, leeks, onions, etc., stink?

Answers:

The answer to question 7 is the Author. For all other answers, read this book!

STOP!
Important Information!
Do not turn the page
until you have read the following:

Alliums:
A group of plants related in a number of ways (reproduction, growth habits, flower types, etc.), but especially by that distinct, glorious, controversial ONIONY smell. Famous alliums include onions, garlic, leeks, chives, and shallots. Lesser known alliums number in the hundreds. Some are stunningly beautiful; some are not so hot. However, they all have in common that aforementioned aroma when crushed or bruised.

Now, if you have read this all the way through like you were supposed to, you'll know what the Author is talking about when she refers to ALLIUMS in the rest of this book.

Okay, now you can turn the page.

1.

HISTORY
AND
LORE

Where would civilization be without the onion?
A French Chef

Pick up an onion. You are holding a universe in your hand. You may not realize that, but an Egyptian living four thousand years ago would have. In ancient Egypt, the onion was considered, and possibly worshipped as, a symbol of the universe—round and layered in concentric circles, as the Egyptians pictured it. Looking at an onion—or a head of garlic, a leek, a bunch of chives—is like looking at the history of the world. So have another look and let's time-travel.

The onion and its relatives were born approximately five thousand years ago probably in the Mid-East or the Mediterranean region.

Moslem legend says that when Satan left the Garden of Eden in triumph after Adam's fall, onions sprang up in his right footprint, garlic in his left. Whether or not that's true, garlic, leeks and onions are mentioned in the oldest of written history—Assyrian and Babylonian tablets, Egyptian papyri, Chinese books—as well as in ancient paintings. In Sumer, where writing was perhaps born, archaeologists unearthed a tablet bearing a citizen's complaint against the *ishakku*, or local bureaucrat, who took everything for himself, as politicians are sometimes wont to do: "The oxen of the gods plowed the *ishakku's* onion patches; the onion and cucumber patches of the *ishakku* were located in the gods' best fields." Chives also most likely came from the Mid-East; they were introduced to China at least two thousand years ago. And shallots, a form of aggregate onion also known as *Allium ascalonicum,* which have never been found in the wild state, may or may not have come from Ascalon, a city in Judaea where they were cultivated. However, they probably date back to the beginning of the first century, A.D.

All of the early civilizations used the alliums medicinally—something we'll get into in a later chapter—but onions, garlic, leeks and all had other important uses, too. The Egyptian pyramid-builders (and, in fact, the Egyptian populace

in general, except possibly for the priests, although they too probably indulged) ate onions as
a wholesome, inexpensive, stamina-providing
food.

Peace Agreement Breakfasts

Egyptian
One or two raw onions or scallions
Several radishes
Bread

Israeli
One or two raw onions or scallions
Several radishes
Bread

The great Greek historian Herodotus wrote
that in his time there was an inscription on the
Great Pyramid, built by Cheops in 2900 B.C.,
that the sum spent for the onions, radishes and
garlic eaten by the laborers in twenty years
amounted to sixteen thousand talents or over
two-hundred-thousand dollars! And the first recorded sit-down strike, which was held at the
Necropolis in Thebes, occurred because the
onion (and other food) wages hadn't been paid
by the government for two months.

According to *The Bible*, garlic, leeks and
onions were some of the foods the Israelites

missed when they left Egypt to wander in the wilderness. In the Passover *seder,* leeks or scallions may be used as *karpas*—spring greens which stand for the bounty of God and of earth. Garlic, however, is forbidden during Passover by some Jewish people, among them the Chasids and certain Poles, because it is said to hasten the fermentation of food.

A Good Jewish Dish— Eggs and Onions (Serves 4)

8 *hard-boiled eggs*	*Salt and black pepper*
1-2 *large Spanish*	⅓ *cup melted butter*
onions	*Parsley for garnish*

Chop the eggs and onions finely. Mix together with the butter. Season with salt and pepper to taste. Serve with parsley garnish, crackers or black and rye breads. You can also add other vegetables to the mixture, such as ½ cup celery or carrots. Garlic is good blended in, too. Or try this variation:

8 *hard-boiled eggs*	1 *cup chopped mixed*
2 *large Spanish*	*nuts, unsalted*
onions	8 *tablespoons tomato*
1½ *cups of butter*	*sauce*
Salt and black pepper	

Chop the eggs (and nuts, if not already chopped) and set aside. Finely chop the onion and fry in the butter until golden. Add the eggs, nuts, salt and pepper to taste. Mix in the tomato sauce and cook until it's hot enough. Then serve with black or rye breads.

In Egypt and other Middle-Eastern civilizations, garlic was also a bartering commodity. For fifteen pounds of garlic, an aristocrat could buy a "healthy" male slave. Women and children were somewhat cheaper. Leeks were used as a type of payment, as shown in this ancient reference: ". . . fix his allowance at a thousand loaves of bread, a hundred jars of beer, one ox and a hundred bunches of leeks."

Onions were also identified with the teeth of the god Horus and given as an offering to him and to other gods. And they were used in the mummification process.

TALES FROM THE TOMB
or
The Mummy's Onion

The passage was long and dark. Nevertheless, Dr. Schreck and his companion,

Max, marched staunchly behind their torch-bearing guide until they came to the burial chamber.

"Here it is, Max," said Dr. Schreck. "What we've been searching for all these years!"

Straining, the men pulled away the heavy ornate gate and entered the room. The guide's torchlight fell first upon the glittering objects strewn about the walls and floor.

"Holy pharaoh!" exclaimed Max. "What a treasure trove!"

"Never mind that," said Dr. Schreck impatiently. "Look at this!" He gestured at the heavy, painted sarcophagus in the center of the room.

"Holy Nefertiti, let's open it," Max shouted.

The guide shrunk back in fear. "No. No! The curse!" His teeth chattered.

"Nonsense!" said Dr. Schreck, and he strode over to the sarcophagus and carefully pried open the lid.

The guide fell gibbering to the floor.

Dr. Schreck felt his pulse. "I think we shall have to find our own way back, Max," he said, and turned back to opening the lid of the inner coffin.

Eventually, it too came off.

"My word!" ejaculated Dr. Schreck, staring into the box after the third and final lid had come away.

"Holy Moses!" cried Max, brandishing the

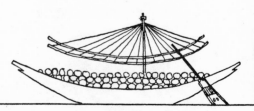

torch. "The mummy... it's clutching an... an ..."

"An onion," finished Dr. Schreck.

And suddenly, the torch went out.

Lightning blazed in the windows. Thunder shook the house. And Dr. Schreck slept uneasily. Alliums haunted his dreams. And he seemed to sense a supernatural presence nearing.

Yet, he did not hear the front doorknob turn and the dragging footsteps that scraped up the stairs.

Nearer and nearer came the steps. A bandaged hand pushed open Dr. Schreck's bedroom door. Still nearer. The hand reached for Schreck's throat.

The doctor's eyes snapped open. He saw the wrapped thing before him, and he screamed.

The mummy clapped his hand over Schreck's mouth until the doctor stopped shrieking. His sightless eyes bored into Schreck's.

There was a long silence.

"Wh... wh... what is it you want?" Schreck finally stammered.

"Hdw," the mummy whispered.

"Pardon?" asked Schreck.

"Hdw," the mummy repeated, louder this time.

"I'm sorry," Schreck said, "but I simply do not understand you."

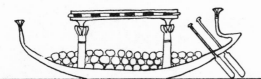

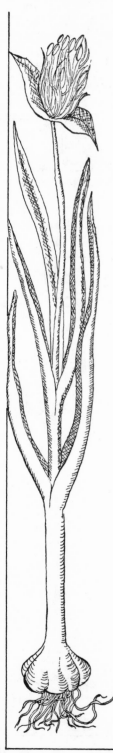

8

Then the mummy shook Schreck fiercely and roared, "Give me back my onion!"
"Here," squeaked Schreck. "Take it!"

Onions, as well as garlic, have actually been found on mummies or in their hands. Garlic was found in Tut's tomb. Onions have also been found in the pelvis, the thorax, the outer ears and behind the eyelids of mummies. They were used freely in the process of embalming in the XX, XXI and XXII dynasties. Rameses IV had onions behind his lids to simulate eyes. Onion skins too were sometimes placed over the eyes of the dead. Also found in the tombs were clay and wooden models of garlic which became "real" through magic rites. Why were onions and garlic used in mummies and their tombs? No one is sure, but it was probably because of the powerful antiseptic, hence "magical," properties onions exhibit. How were they used in mummification? Here for your edification are the fifteen steps to making a mummy:

1. After the body has been taken to the Per-nefer or House of Mummification, remove the clothing and place it, naked, on a large wooden board.
2. Remove the brain through the nose (this takes great skill).

3. Remove all the innards (that's the guts) except for the kidneys. Remove all the contents of the thoracic cavity (chest) except for the heart.

4. Wash the chest and abdominal cavities thoroughly with palm wine and spices.

5. Wash the innards separately and place in a container of natron (a natural compound of sodium bicarbonate and sodium chloride or sulphate) for forty days. Then sprinkle the guts with perfume, treat with hot resin, wrap in packages and place in four canopic jars.

6. Stuff the chest and abdominal cavities with a temporary material (sand, straw, resin, rags, dried vegetable fibers, etc.) to speed dehydration and prevent disfiguration of the body.

7. Place the body on a sloping board and cover with heaps of dried natron.

8. After approximately forty days, when dehydration has taken place, remove the natron and the temporary stuffing. Set the stuffing aside. Wash the body thoroughly with water and palm wine. Dry carefully.

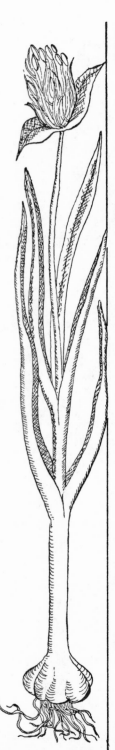

9. Place into the skull cavity resin or resin-soaked linen. In the abdominal cavity, put sawdust, myrrh and ONIONS, all carefully wrapped in separate linen bags. Then, sew up the abdomen.
10. Rub the body with a mixture of cedar oil, cumin, wax, natron, gum, milk and wine. Dust with spices.
11. To give a lifelike appearance to the face, pad the cheeks (inside) with linen. Plug the nose. And use linen or ONIONS in the eye sockets and close the lids.
12. Coat the body with molten resin to strengthen the skin and prevent moisture from entering.
13. Paint the eyebrows. Place jewelry on the body. Bandage by separately wrapping each finger and toe, then each arm and leg, and finally, the whole body. Put an ONION in the mummy's hand.
14. Put everything that touched the mummy during these thirteen steps into 67 large pots and bury near the tomb.
15. Lay the mummy in its coffin, then

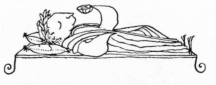

into a second coffin, and finally, into
the sarcophagus and carry to the tomb.
NOTE: Onions were not used in every mummy,
nor were all of the other stuffings.
SECOND NOTE: Do not attempt mummification
unless you are a genuine, qualified Ancient
Egyptian.

Whoever has eaten garlic knows its smell.

Popular Middle-Eastern saying

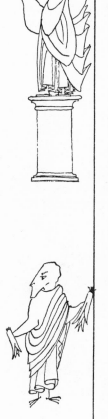

Juvenal, the Roman satirist, is largely responsible for some of our misconceptions about
Egyptians and alliums. It was he who claimed
that the Egyptians swore oaths on onions and
that priests did not eat them. There is little
evidence on the latter, save for some other Roman
writings. As for swearing on onions, that may or
may not have been because alliums were worshipped. More likely, such an oath was taken
because the onion, or garlic, is a *divine blessing*—
food from the good gods—to be forfeited if the
oath were not kept. In other words, this oath
would be like saying, "May God take the bread
from my mouth if I don't marry you!", or whatever
the particular vow happens to be.

And furthermore, there is no doubt that
alliums were thought to be a divine blessing, as
this story goes to show:

An ancient Arabian tale tells of a king who was so delighted by the gift of an onion, the first he had ever seen, that he gave the blessed man who presented him with this rare treasure a fortune in gold and jewels. This lucky traveller continued on his way and told the story of his luck to the next man he met. As fate would have it, that man had a head of garlic he had intended to plant.

Ah, he thought, if the king so liked the onion, how much more would he enjoy this potent bulb! Then, he fell into a dream about the fortune that would come his way. But I shall not ask for gold or jewels, he said to himself. Instead I shall ask for a house with a garden around it. And in the garden I will plant garlic to sell—so much garlic I will be able to buy the whole kingdom!

Quickly, he sent word to the king. And just as quickly he was summoned to the king's royal chamber.

"Ah, so you are here at last," said the king, "And you bear with you the most precious thing in the world."

A small smile crossed the man's lips. He wiped it away and nodded as humbly as he could.

"Well then, let me see it," said the king.

With a deft movement, the man produced the garlic. He bowed and placed it in the king's hand.

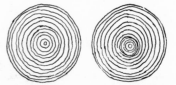

The king turned it over. He sniffed the bulb. Then, he peeled off a clove and bit into it. "Ah," he exclaimed, "Truly a treasure!"

The man smiled again.

"For this, you shall have my own most cherished possession." Then, he clapped his hands and sent his chamberlain to fetch the prize.

And all the while, the man smiled and bowed.

And finally, the chamberlain returned carrying something on a blue silk cushion.

"Here, my friend, is your reward," said the king.

And he gave the man a fine fat onion.

Then, the man bowed once more and went home. But this time, he was not smiling.

Nor, as mentioned before, is there any doubt that alliums were used in divine rites—mummification being one of these. Some Egyptologists feel onions may have been put into mummies or their tombs to stimulate the dead to breathe in the afterlife. In the Sokaris festivals held at the winter solstice in Memphis, participants wore onions around their necks and frequently smelled them—a death and resurrection rite. Today in the Mid-East, on Sham-en-Nassim, Coptic Easter Monday, people eat onions and offer them to friends to smell—a sure way to

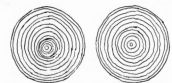

revive, if not the dead, at least those with bad colds. William Darby, Paul Ghalioungui and Louis Grivetti in *Food: The Gift of Osiris* point out that the American equivalent of these rites are the rural "ramp festivals."

Festivals to Take Your (Sweet) Breath Away (and then give it back!)

1. Sham-en-Nassim.
2. Ramp Festivals. These take place in many parts of the U.S., particularly in the Southeast. In Cosby, Tennessee, on the fourth Sunday in April, a Ramp Festival has been dedicated to "the sweetest tasting and vilest smelling plant that grows"—the *ramson* or wild onion. Everyone eats his or her fill of this delectable herb, sings, dances and celebrates the end of Lent, the coming of long, warm days.
3. To go-a-leeking. The European ramp festival. Anyone can participate. Simply enter a forest in spring with a shaker of salt and a good appetite.

See p. 99 for other festivals.

Now, back to ancient Egypt. Besides use in holy rites, alliums, particularly garlic, were im-

portant in other magical practices, such as the making of charms and the casting of spells. Here are two spells, without the incantations, from *The Leyden Papyrus*, an Egyptian magical text:

(*To summon a deity*) "... on the third day of the month, there being a three-lobed white garlic and there being three needles of iron piercing it, and recite this to it... seven times; and put it at thy head. Then he attends to you and speaks with you."

(*A spell spoken in the name of Isis to heal the bite of a dog*). "And you pound garlic with *kmou* [?] and you put it on the wound of the bite of the dog; and you address it daily until it is well."

Alliums and magic—a potent combination found in many cultures, past and present. In Babylon, Marduk, the chief god, learned how to use onions to remove a curse:

> Go, my son Marduk,
> Take him to the pure ablution-house,
> Loose his spell, loose his spell,
> That the activating evil of his body, whether the
> curse of his father, or the curse of his mother, or
> the curse of his elder brother, or the curse of the
> murder of a man he does not know,
> By the conjuration of Ea,
> Let the curse be peeled off like this onion,

Let it be wrenched apart like this date,
Let it be untwined like this wick.

For each of these objects—onion, date, wick—there was a separate incantation. For the onion, it went:

Like this onion which he peels and throws into the fire, which the fire consumes entirely, . . . whose roots will not take hold in the soil, whose shoots will not sprout, that will not be used for the meal of a god or a king, so may oath, curse . . . sickness, weariness, guilt, sin, wickedness, transgression, the sickness that is in my body, my flesh or my limbs, be peeled off like this onion; may the fire consume it entirely today; may the curse be taken away that I may see the light.

Small wonder that as alliums spread to the Far East, to Europe and then to the Americas, they have been invested with supernatural abilities from destroying a magnet's power (try it and see if it works!) to making a heartthrob fall in love with you to chasing away evil spirits. Before we continue our odoriferous history, here is:

A MAGICKAL ALLIACEOUS MYSTERY TOUR[1] with Much Ado About Botanomancy[2]

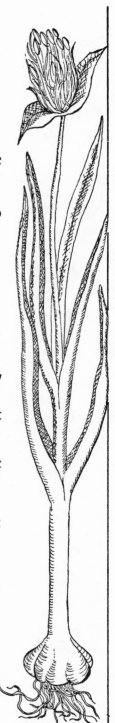

Middle East
A clove of garlic worn in the buttonhole of the bridegroom insures a happy wedding night.

Carry garlic cloves in a blue velvet cushion to ward off evil.

Europe
How to win a race:
Chew garlic when you are about to run a race, and your competitors will never get ahead of you.

Mediterranean Region
To ward off the evil eye, say, "Garlic in your eye!"

Cloves of garlic carried by sailors will avert shipwreck.

If anyone utters praise with the intention of harming you, cry, "Garlic!"

To save a son from illness or death, place garlic near the father's bed and the boy will live.

1 The author has not tested these charms, so they may or may not work.
2 Botanomancy—divination or fortune-telling using plants.

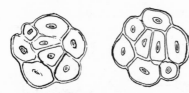

Spain

Bullfighters carry garlic to prevent the bull from charging.

How to get rid of someone you're not interested in:
Choose a spot where two roads cross. On the ground place two crossed pins and a piece of garlic. Get the person in question to walk over the charm and he/she will never bother you again.

Spanish women carry garlic in their pockets to keep witches away. The bulb is discarded only when it has lost its magical powers from rubbing against the metal coins in the same pocket.

Italy

Bolognese regard garlic as a symbol of abundance and buy it on Midsummer Night (June 23) as a charm against poverty.

How to tell if a person far away is in good health:
On Christmas Eve, take onions and put them on an altar. Under every onion, write the name of the person you want to know about. The onion which sprouts first will clearly announce that the person whose name it bears is well.

Hungary

How to win a horse race:
Fasten a clove of garlic to the horse's bit. When

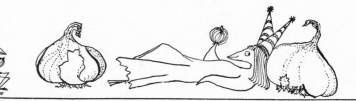

the other horses smell the garlic, they will fall back.

Gypsy

How to get someone you are interested in to like you back:
In a clean pot, never before used, plant an onion. While you do this, repeat the name of the one you love. Then, every day, morning and evening, say over it:

> *As this root grows*
> *And as this blossom blows*
> *May her (his) heart be*
> *Turned unto me!*

And you will win your love.

A charm to thwart Chagrin, the Gypsy demon who torments horses:
Tie the horse to a stake rubbed with garlic juice. Lay red thread in the form of a cross on the ground far enough from the horse so he or she cannot disturb it. While laying the cross, chant:

> *All evil stay here,*
> *Stay in the long thread,*
> *In the next brook*
> *Give thy water,*
> *Jump in Chagrin!*
> *Therein perish quickly!*

How to keep your horse in good spirits during the waning moon:
Rub his/her spine with garlic and say:

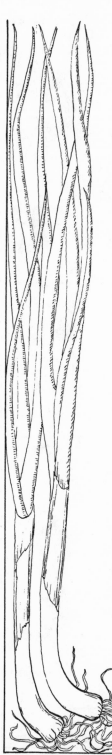

(What is) evil in thee,
May the devil eat it much!
(What is) good in thee,
May it remain in thee!

Gypsies use chives in fortune-telling (although the Author has not been able to find out how) and to ward off disease. For the latter, chives are suspended from ceilings and bedposts.

Germany/Bohemia
Give garlic to dogs, cocks and ganders to make them fearless and strong.

Miners used garlic against impure spirits in the mines.

Scandinavia
The Elder Edda, the oldest Norse mythology, says that garlic exorcises evil spirits.

Great Britain
To protect a bride from the Evil Eye:
Throw an onion after her as she leaves the church.

To keep away fairies, witches and other malevolent spirits from newborn babies:
Between birth and baptism, put garlic in the baby's cradle.

Onions are sacred to St. Thomas, whose day is

December 21![1] At old holiday celebrations, a young man representing the Saint would give each girl in the group a quarter of an onion. She would then whisper to it the name of the young man she loved, wave the onion above her head and recite this spell:

> *Good Saint Thomas do me right,*
> *and send me my true love come tonight.*
> *That I may see him in the face, and him*
> *in my kind arms embrace.*

If the girl got to bed by midnight, she was sure to dream of her loved one.

In Britain, another good day to dream, via alliums, of a loved one—in this case, a future husband—is St. Agnes' Eve, January 20 (read the poem "The Eve of St. Agnes" by John Keats and you'll see). For the unmarried female readers who would like to try it, here is the formula:

Boil a kettle of salted water and drop in three garlic bulbs. Simmer for ½ hour; then remove the garlic. Eat one clove from each of the bulbs and take the remaining portions to your bed. Tuck under your pillow. Then, climb in and say:

> *Dear St. Agnes, hear my plea*
> *Garlic keeps evil from thee,*
> *Visit me with a dream tonight*

---

1 Now July 3, according to the recent revision of the Roman liturgical calendar.

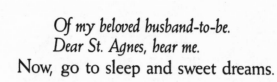

Of my beloved husband-to-be.
Dear St. Agnes, hear me.
Now, go to sleep and sweet dreams.

Yet another technique to find the right mate:
Scratch the names of four possible boyfriends on
each of four onions and put in a dark place. The
first to sprout shows the name of the winner.

*One for boys about to be caned (a British form of corporal
punishment in which students who act up get beaten on the
hand or elsewhere with a hard cane):*
Rub raw onion on the palm to deaden the pain of
the stroke. Or, better still, if possible, rub it on
the cane itself, and it will split as soon as it is
used.

Bolivia
Bolivian Indians believe a bull won't charge a
person carrying garlic.

Haiti and the West Indies
A voodoo charm:
Put pieces of garlic in a red flannel sack and tie
around your neck to keep away evil spirits.

Puerto Rico
For good luck and wealth, hang a bulb of garlic
on a green ribbon in the doorway.

Southern U.S.
An onion carried on the left side keeps away

disease. An onion burned in a fire brings good luck.

Unspecified locales

Another love charm:
Take two garlic bulbs and fasten them together with a steel nail. The top bulb stands for the person making the charm, the bottom one for the desired sweetie. Hide the charm in the corner of a dark closet until the loved one responds.

A bath for warding off evil:
Blend seven small pieces of garlic; seven dry basil leaves; seven shakes of dried parsley; seven shakes of dried sage; seven drops of geranium oil; a pinch of thyme; and a pinch of saltpeter with some of your bathwater. Pour a bit in each bath you take on Tuesday, Thursday and Saturday. After bathing fourteen minutes, dry off completely and rub down thoroughly with bay rum. Then, rub down again with verbena oil or perfume. This will remove any hex and prevent any others from occurring for seven weeks.

A bath to purify you:
Boil one whole garlic bulb and one ounce of thyme in five gallons of water for one hour. Then, put it in your bath and soak. Believe it or not, the garlic deodorizes!

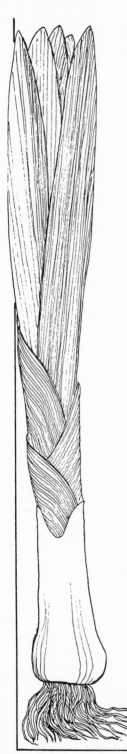

A spring cleaning recipe:
Leave half an onion in a newly painted room to cleanse the air of impurities.

China
"He who wears a clove of garlic need not fear the evil eye."

Which ends our tour and brings us neatly to the Orient, where the alliums were next to go from the Middle East (although there is some disagreement on this).

The alliums have been—and are—very important in many Eastern countries. Garlic is mentioned in the oldest surviving Chinese text—*Shih Ching* or *The Book of Songs* (600 B.C.). Yoshio Kato, a Japanese garlic expert, says garlic entered China during the Han Dynasty (130-120 B.C.) when Emperor Wu-ti sent Chang Chien to the silk route areas to establish cultural and diplomatic relations and that the latter returned with garlic and other vegetables. It was later found that a different species of garlic already grew in China. Kato says the two crossed into one species. Others claim garlic was written about almost 4,000 years ago in China. But whatever is correct, garlic—*suan*—has long been a chief ingredient in Chinese cooking and medicine, with Shantung province being the center of

garlicky cuisine; and it is eaten by everyone except Buddhist priests. In the 13th century, Marco Polo watched people eating raw meat in garlic sauce—a marinade which preserves and detoxifies the meat. A Chinese cookbook from the same period mentions a dish called "Colored Rice from the West" that contains mutton, garlic, saffron and rice and is very healthful. A mid-16th century herbal includes the cultivation and uses of garlic.

Chinese or Italian Broccoli and Garlic
(Why not? The Chinese introduced spaghetti, didn't they?)

One bunch broccoli	3 tablespoons olive
3-4 cloves garlic,	oil or peanut oil
chopped coarsely	¼ teaspoon sugar
	(Chinese version)

Cut up the broccoli and steam it until tender/ crisp. Drain. Fry the garlic in the oil (olive for Italian style, peanut for Chinese). Don't overcook it. Add sugar for Chinese style. Put in the broccoli and stir-fry until it's hot and well-coated. Serves 4.

Scallions and a variety of leeks were eaten by the commoners—often the poor—in the

Orient, and so came to mean "humility." But, there were times when they were not so readily available. In 33 B.C., Shao Hsin-Ch'en got permission from Emperor Yuan to close down an imperial greenhouse for the cultivation of out-of-season vegetables including scallions and leeks. The latter were also important as an offering during the First Moon to ancestors. They were also mentioned in numerous herbals—not always favorably. In *Yin-Shih hsü-chih* (1368), Chia Ming writes of leeks:

Eaten in the spring season, they are fragrant and quite beneficial. Eaten in the summer, they are malodorous. Eaten in the winter, they cause a person to arise during the Fifth Moon; they cause a person to become dizzy and weak.

On the other hand, later herbals such as Li Shih-Chen's *Pen-ts'ao Kang-mu* (1590) attest to the leek's wonderful medicinal properties:

It restores the spirit and calms the five viscera, eliminates fever in the stomach, and benefits a sick person. It can be eaten over a long period of time.

Today, in New York's Chinatown, the streets are redolent with scallions, leeks and other alliums. You can even find a dessert cake called *hopia baboy* which is filled with onions and winter melon (a squash).

Chives too have been valued in China as an antidote to poison, a remedy to bleeding and a tasty addition to many a dish. They also, recently, gave the Chinese language a new phrase, "chive-cutting mentality," meaning the attitude of those who, in early Communist days, feared that anything they got of worth would be taken and redistributed just as the chives that stick up above the others get cut first.

From China, the alliums spread to Korea where they have enhanced the cuisine for many years. In addition, onions and garlic have a special place in Korean mythology. In the story of "Dan-Gun, First King of Korea," the Heavenly Prince, Hwan-Ung, comes to earth under the sacred sandalwood tree and there rules. A bear and a tiger living in a cave near the tree wish desperately to become human. Every day, they pray to the Prince until he is moved by their sincerity. He gives them twenty bulbs of garlic and a bundle of mugwort (an herb related to wormwood) and says, "Eat these and confine yourselves deep in your cave for one hundred days, and then you will become human." So, the bear and the tiger take the garlic and the mugwort and enter their cave. Eventually, the tiger becomes tired of the long, dark days and leaves, but the bear patiently endures weariness and hunger and boredom. And, after twenty-one days, she becomes a beautiful woman who, in turn, becomes the bride of the Heavenly Prince and gives birth to Dan-Gun, the Sandalwood King.

A second story involving alliums is told here by Korean folklorist Zŏng Yŏng-Ha:

In the very earliest days of human history, there was a time when men used to eat one another. This was because in those days men often appeared in the form of cattle, and so were slaughtered for food.

At last a certain man set out in quest of a better world. In his wanderings he met a leper, who asked him the reason for his journey. He answered, "This world is horrible and I hate it, for men eat one another. I am on my way to seek a better world, where men may not do such evil things."

To this the leper replied, "Your quest will be in vain, for wherever you may go you will find that men everywhere behave in the same way. So I would advise you to go back to your native place."

Then the wanderer replied, "I cannot go back now, for if I do they will assuredly kill me. Whatever shall I do?"

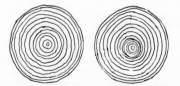

The leper said, "My advice to you is that you should eat onions. Any man who does so will thereafter appear in human form, even though he has previously appeared in the form of an ox."

So then the traveller hastened homewards. As he drew near his home, he met some of his friends, and greeted them cheerfully, "Hello, how do you do? I haven't seen you for some time."

Thereupon the others said, "The lowing of this ox is most remarkable," and instantly they seized him.

He was greatly alarmed, and said, "No, I am not an ox. I am your friend, and my name is..."

But the others did not understand what he was saying, and said to one another, "This ox is bellowing too much. Isn't he making a din? We had better kill him at once." With these words they tied him to a post.

Just then it happened that a young girl passed by, carrying a basket full of onions on her head. With a great effort he managed to snatch one and swallow it. When he had eaten it all, he immediately changed into human form. The others were astonished, and said, "What, so it is you, our dear friend. We are very sorry indeed. We did not realize it was you."

So then he told them all about the miraculous powers of onions and advised them to eat them. From that day men began to eat

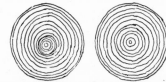

onions, and thereafter always appeared in human form. And it is said that the cultivation of onions was encouraged in order that men might not eat one another any more.

These lovely tales show the high regard the Korean people have held for the fabulous alliums. Garlic, leeks, onions and chives are also mentioned extensively in Korean poetry and other literature.

Allium Sativum Pickles

Separate the cloves of several heads of garlic. Soak in salted water for a week. Remove the skins from the cloves, put them in a Mason jar and cover them with a mixture of vinegar and sugar. Seal the jar and let it stand undisturbed for six months. You may use soy sauce instead of vinegar for pickling.

Garlic got to Japan via Korea around 30 B.C. It is described in *Kojiki*, the Japanese historical record, in some poems in *Manyoshu*, and in *Utsubo-Monogatari*, where the author describes the delicious taste of garlic cooked with fish. In the famous 11th century *Tale of the Genji* by Lady Murosaki, the earliest Japanese novel, a character, the daughter of a noted scholar, catches a cold and takes garlic as a remedy. Her lover comes to visit, but is put off by the odor. Leaving, he says, "Come to talk to me when you become free from that smell."

It seems the upper classes in a lot of places were not great garlic devotees. Actually, Kato says that the aristocracy in Japan did not always dislike garlic. In feudal times, it was highly prized by the samurai, or professional soldiers, for its medical properties. But centuries later when Japan conquered China, Russia and Korea in the latter half of the Meiji Era, it began to look down on the habits and foods of these nations. And, as we've seen, one of these foods was garlic. However, this disdain also seems linked to the introduction of Buddhism into Japan. So much was this herb frowned upon then that the old Korean word for garlic—*hiru*—was replaced in Japanese by *ninniku*, "to endure insults." Garlic-eaters were shunned because of the odor and for the belief by many cultures, Greek, Roman, Jewish and Japanese among them, that garlic was an *aphrodisiac*—a substance that causes sexual arousal. Therefore, persons who indulged in eating it were thought to be oversexed. A Buddhist priest who reeked of garlic was an immediate prey to dirty jokes! So priests were ordered to refrain from eating it.

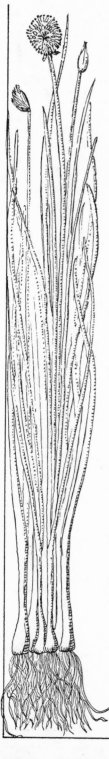

Perhaps this taboo came from prohibitions in earlier cultures, such as Babylon:

IN THE MONTH OF TASHRIT...
first day:... (a man) shall not eat garlic, or a scorpion will sting him; he shall not eat an onion, or there will be dysentery (in store) for him...;
second day: he shall not eat garlic, or an important person in his family will die; ...he shall not ascend to a roof, or the Handmaid of Lilu will espouse him.

The alliums have been and are banned by other cultures, too, as being rude and unfit for the spiritual life. In India, *tamasic* or taboo foods include "garlic, onions, also leeks and mushrooms" which, according to the ordinances of Manu (6th century, B.C.) "are not to be eaten by the twice-born, as well as things arising from impurity." Brahmins, Hindu widows and Jains do not touch them. In Southern India, for the other devout Hindus, onions are banned for four months of the year.

But for the remaining eight months, watch out! Onions and garlic are among the staples of Indian cooking and medicine. There is even a curry called "Do Piyaz" or "Do Piaza," which literally translates "Two Onions."

An Oniony Indian Dish—Tari Aloo

½ cup vegetable oil

1 teaspoon black
   mustard seeds

2 tablespoons finely
   chopped fresh ginger

1 fresh green chili
   pepper, seeded and
   chopped fine

1 tablespoon ground
   coriander

1 teaspoon turmeric

½ teaspoon paprika

4 cups potatoes, boiled,
   peeled and cut into
   small cubes

3 cups chopped onions

4 cups water

1¼ tablespoons salt

2 teaspoons lemon juice

3-4 tablespoons chopped
   coriander leaves

Heat the oil over high heat in a deep pan or wok. When the oil is very hot, carefully add the mustard seeds and cover as the seeds "pop." When the seeds stop popping and turn gray, which only takes a minute or two, reduce the heat slightly and add the ginger and chili. Cook for two or three minutes. Then, add everything except for the last six ingredients. Stir, and add the potatoes and onions. Saute for ten minutes, stirring frequently. Add four cups of water and sprinkle the mixture with salt. Cover and simmer for about 15 minutes. Stir in the lemon juice. Sprinkle with the chopped coriander leaves. Serve with Indian style bread. Serves 8.

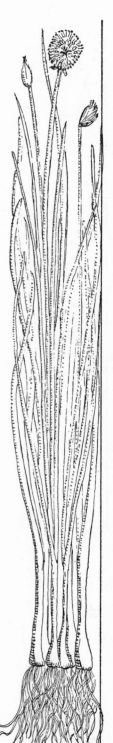

Persian and Indian Zoroastrians, who believe that two forces (one good, one evil) are forever at war over the hearts of men, have a holiday called Sir-Sava, the Garlic Feast, when they consume mass quantities to keep away evil spirits. They rank with the great allium-eaters of the world. But there are lots of others.

GREAT ALLIUM-EATERS OF THE WORLD
or
"Lovers live by love, as larks by leeks."

1. John Harris (formerly Lloyd J. Harris), Head Garlichead of Lovers of the Stinking Rose, founder of *Garlic Times* and author of *The Book of Garlic.*
2. Sancho Panza (see *Don Quixote*), who preferred garlic to being a governor.
3. Eleanor Roosevelt, who claimed that her super memory and energy were due to exercise, vitamins and the three chocolate-coated garlic pills she took regularly.
4. Wood pigeons, which eat onion greens and small bulbs.

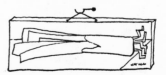

5. Wild allium-devouring white-tailed prairie dogs.

6. Dog-dogs. Although Albertus Magnus, the Medieval scientist, thought, "a Dog tasteth not anything dipped with Garlic, although he be hungry," Albertus Magnus was wrong. Dogs are perhaps the top allium-eaters in the world. In periodic feeding trials, dog food companies found that many canines wouldn't even touch food that did not have garlic in it!

7. The golden-mantled ground squirrel, which eats *Allium haematochiton*, the wild red onion. Also the Columbian ground squirrel.

8. Onion-eating antelopes and giraffes in 19th century English zoos.

9. Chickens. A small piece of garlic chopped fine and put into chickens' food daily *before* they start laying will produce finer eggs. It will also make them lay eggs in any weather. But you must stop feeding them when they begin to lay or you'll have garlic-flavored eggs. Which may not be such a bad thing!

10. Huerfanita (Nita, for short), an onion-eating gorilla at New York's Bronx Zoo.

This way to ancient Greece! ⟶

GREEKS AND LEEKS

As the alliums moved east to China, they also moved west to Greece (some feel they moved first to Greece), where they quickly became popular. The leek/onion was sacred to Leto, Apollo's mother, who, having lost her taste for food because of an illness, ate this fragrant appetite-stimulant and recovered. So, at the festival of Theoxenia at Delphi, at which all the gods were Apollo's guests, whoever brought the largest *gethyllis* (leek/onion) was entitled to a share of the sacrificial feast in Leto's honor. In *The Iliad*, Homer's account of the Trojan War, when Hecamede serves wine to the warriors Nestor and Machaon, she sets before them as a relish an onion on a bronze dish. And the Thracians, from near Greece, supposedly presented onions as wedding gifts.

Leeks a la Grecque

5 cups vegetable stock
1⅓ cups olive oil
Juice of two lemons
2 sticks celery
24 coriander seeds

Bouquet garni
  (herb mixture)
20 peppercorns
12 small leeks
Salt to taste

Simmer the stock with all the ingredients except the leeks and salt for five minutes. While this is cooking, trim and wash the leeks. Then, put them into the liquid, add the salt, cover and cook for twenty minutes or until tender. Let the leeks cool in the liquid. Remove them and place on a dish. Then, reduce the liquid by boiling, cool and spoon it over the leeks. Chill. Other vegetables such as celery, mushrooms, artichoke hearts, zucchini, etc., may be served this way. Serves 4.

A peculiar Greek onion tale involves an invasion and a deception. When the Locrians (Greeks) invaded Italy, they swore they would share the land with the original inhabitants in peace and friendship for as long as they still trod the earth and carried their heads on their shoulders. The poor Italians believed and welcomed them. And then, the Locrians took off their

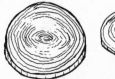

sandals and poured out the dirt. They pulled big onion heads from beneath their tunics. "We no longer tread this earth," they said, pointing to the dirt from their shoes. "We no longer carry our heads on our shoulders," they grinned, waving the onions. And they conquered the Italians and took total possession of the country, prompting the proverb, "The oath of the Locrians!" meaning a phoney oath that is never kept.

A Macedonian Dish—Rice and Leek Casserole

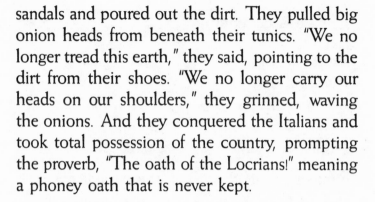

4-5 leeks
¼ cup olive oil
1 teaspoon salt
½ teaspoon cayenne
Pinch of hot red pepper
    flakes, crushed

1 cup rice
1 cup canned tomatoes,
    chopped
1½ cups meat or
    vegetable stock

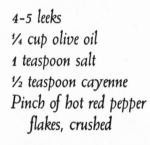

Clean and wash the leeks. Chop and use the white portions. Preheat the oven to 375 degrees. Heat the oil in a large casserole. Add the leeks and simmer for 10 minutes or until tender but not brown. Mix in the salt, cayenne, pepper flakes and rice. Then add the tomatoes and stock and bring to a boil. Cover the casserole and cook in the oven for 20 to 30 minutes, or until the rice is done. Check during the baking to see if more liquid is

needed. Toss lightly and serve. You may also add Parmesan cheese for a more international flavor. Serves 2-4.

Skordalia

2 pounds baking potatoes
5 or more cloves garlic
1½ teaspoons salt

½ cup olive oil
Juice of ½ lemon
Pepper to taste

Peel the potatoes. Cut into cubes. Boil until tender. Drain. Mash. Then, crush the garlic either in a garlic press or in a mortar with a pestle. Mix the garlic and salt into the mashed potatoes. Pour in the olive oil gradually, beating the potatoes the whole time. Add the lemon juice and pepper. Stir. Can be served heated as a side dish or cold as a dip. Serves 4 (or more as a dip).

What would Greek cooking be without garlic? The same might be said for Ancient Greek culture. The Greeks gave garlic to criminals to "purify" them, buried garlic at crossroads for Hecate, goddess of magic, and used garlic as protection against the malicious and jealous Neriades, nymphs who envied happy marriages

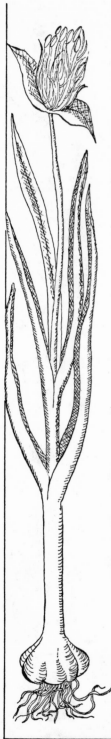

(John Harris tells of a similar Scandinavian creature, the Huldra, who can also be chased off by garlic). In *The Odyssey,* Odysseus is saved from becoming a swine at the hands of another wily woman (the Greeks certainly seemed afraid of females)—the sorceress Circe—by *Allium moly,* a wild garlic. *Rhizotomi,* Greek root gatherers, smeared themselves with garlic oil or ate a lot of garlic before gathering *hellebore,* a poisonous herb, probably as a protection against its deadly juices or perhaps even its aura. And in Aristophanes' *Lysistrata* where the women rebel against their warrior husbands, Cynnali says to Acestor, "If you come near me I swear you'll never eat either garlic or black beans again," an indication of the popularity of the food.

However, garlic was not tops with all Greeks. The nature goddess Cybele apparently detested the odor because garlic-eating Greeks (and Romans) were refused entrance to her temple. Aristocratic Greeks frowned upon its smell. But the common people of Greece did not worry about such niceties, and they continued—and continue—to eat garlic with aplomb. At the present time the Monday before Lent is known in Greece as "Clean Monday." On this day, people picnic on non-meat foods, especially garlic, in a "spring-cleaning" ritual.

GARLIC GOES TO WAR!
(Onions too!)

In late 19th century Greece, to teach the untrained soldiers left and right, the officers tied to each man an onion on one side and a garlic bulb on the other. Then, instead of commanding "Left! Right!" they ordered, "Onion! Garlic! Onion! Garlic!" Hence the expression "Skordokrommede" ("Skorthokrommethe"), translated "Garlic-Onion," but meaning to march left and right.

That is a true story—not a joke. Here are the jokes:

GARLICKY GIGGLES

Two secretaries for an insurance company were having lunch. One of them had been reading up on death rates.

"Did you know that every time I breathe a man dies?" she said.

"That's what I've been telling you," answered the other. "You shouldn't eat so much garlic!"

Onions are funny. Garlic and leeks are, too. At least that's what people throughout history have felt, because allium jokes are as old as the hills.

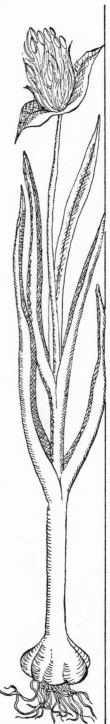

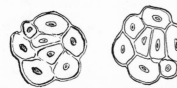

The First Great Garlic Joke

Oma looma tooma.
Begga begga begga.
Oma tooma garlic.
Yuk. Yuk.

The First Great Onion Joke

(From *The Banquet* by Xenophon, written over 2,000 years ago)

Nicerates: . . . the same Homer says somewhere that an onion goes well with a bottle. Now let some of your servants bring an onion, and you will see with what pleasure you will drink.

Charmides: I know very well what he means; Nicerates, gentlemen, thinks deeper than you imagine. He would willingly go home with the smell of an onion in his mouth, that his wife may not be jealous, or suspect he has been kissing someone else.

Socrates: A very good thought, but perhaps I have one as whimsical and worthy of him: it is, that an onion does not only go well with wine, but with food too, and gives a greater seasoning; but if you should eat them now after supper, they would say we had an orgy at Callias'.

Callias: No, no, you can never think so; for onions, they say, are very good to prepare people for the day of battle and inspire courage; you know they feed cocks so they should fight

well; but our business, at present, is love, not war; and so much for onions.

An Early Onion Joke

(From the 13th century *Romance of the Rose* by Guillaume de Lorris and Jean de Meun) The lover who can't cry enough to arouse his beloved's pity is advised to "get an onion or a leek" and he'll be able to produce plenty of tears.

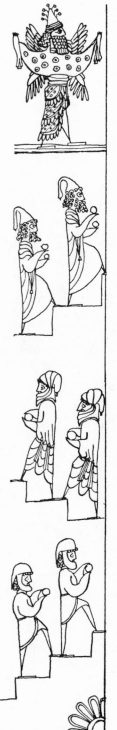

This joke is thereafter found in innumerable plays and novels, including Shakespeare's *The Taming of the Shrew*:

> (Prologue) *And if the boy have not a woman's gift*
> *To rain a shower of commended tears,*
> *An onion will do well for such a shift*
> *Which in a napkin being well*
> *concealed*
> *Shall in despite enforce a wat'ry eye.*

The lachrymatory (tear-producing) quality of onions is a standard of jokedom. Also from Shakespeare (*All's Well That Ends Well*): "*Mine eyes smell onions, I/Shall weep anon.*"

So is the smelly quality... In Shakespeare's *A Midsummer Night's Dream*, Bottom tells his working class companions who are to perform for the court: "*Eat no onions nor garlic, for we are to utter sweet breath...*"

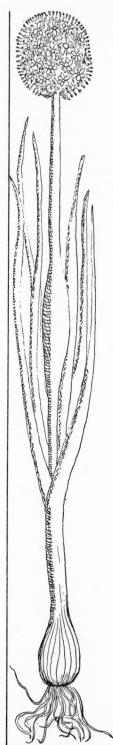

And Shakespeare's contemporary, Francis Bacon, wrote of a poor fellow living for days on the smell of garlic alone.

And then there's this silly verse:

If leeks you like but do their smell disleek
Eate onyons and you shalle not smelle the leeke.
If you of onyons would the scent expelle
Eate garlicke, that shalle drowne the onyon's smelle.

On a more modern note:
Some people think the secret of health lies in eating onions, but the problem is keeping it a secret.

Or this one:
Mary: Why do you feed your kids garlic at bedtime?
Joan: So we can find them in the dark.

Or how about:
Moe: How's that mean dog of yours?
Joe: Oh, he's a lot better. I've been feeding him garlic.
Moe: Garlic?
Joe: Yep—and now his bark is worse than his bite.

That's all, folks!

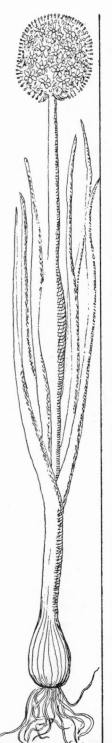

THE ALLIUM EXPANSION
or
Rome Wasn't Built in a Day

A Roman Housekeeping Account, 1 A.D.

	Obols (monetary unit)
February 4—lunch for the weaver	1
Pure bread for the children	½
Beer for the weaver	2
Leeks for the weaver's lunch	1

Like the Greeks whom they copied, the Romans were great allium-eaters (and like the Greek upper classes, some Roman aristocrats sneered at the herbs). They dedicated garlic to Mars, god of war, and fed it to soldiers, horses, fighting cocks, etc. Pliny, the Roman naturalist, wrote of numerous remedies using the alliums (61 with garlic, 32 with leeks). He even claimed that wild garlic could be used to capture birds. Boil it and throw it to the birds to eat the seeds, he said, and this will numb them so they can be caught by hand.

Garlic and onions were very much the food of warriors, the working class and the poor. The poet Alexis comments on the latter in a poem about a family of five:

Yet, alas! Alas! have we
Nourishment for only three!
Two must therefore often make
Scanty meal on barley cake...
And our best and daintiest cheer,
Throughout the bright half of the year,
Is but acorns, beans, chick-peas,
Cabbages, lupins, radishes
Onions, wild pears nine or ten
And a grasshopper now and then.

But the aristocracy did indulge. In his high-class cookbook, Apicius includes many allium recipes, usually using *liquamen*, a sauce of salted fish entrails the Romans seem to have poured into almost everything. Here's his "Puree of Lettuce-leaves with Onions":

Boil the lettuce and onions in water with cooking soda; drain; chop finely. Pound in a mortar, pepper, lovage, celery seed, dried mint and onion; add *liquamen*, oil and wine. Mix with lettuce and onions and serve.

Sounds putrid, doesn't it? But then again, we're not Romans.

Two Italian recipes that don't sound putrid:

Garlic Spaghetti

1 pound spaghetti   *¼ cup olive oil*
10 cloves garlic

Boil the spaghetti *al dente* (until just done).
Chop the garlic coarsely. Fry it in the oil, but
don't let it brown. Drain the spaghetti. Mix the
garlic/oil with the spaghetti. Serves 4.

Tomatoes and Onions Gorgonzola

2-4 large ripe tomatoes   *Salt and pepper*
1 large Bermuda or   *¼ pound gorgonzola*
Spanish onion   *cheese at room*
1 tablespoon red wine   *temperature*
vinegar   *(you may substitute*
3 tablespoons olive oil   *bleu or roquefort*
                                 cheese)

Slice the tomatoes. Peel and slice the onion.
Arrange decoratively on a platter. In a mixing
bowl, blend the vinegar, oil, salt and pepper to
taste. Add the cheese and mix well into the
other ingredients (the dressing should be
slightly lumpy). Pour over the tomatoes and
onions. Serves 4.

The juice of leeks who
  fondly sips,
To kiss the fair must close
  his lips.

Martial (or anonymous)

Of the alliums, leeks were especially popular in ancient Rome. And for all his warning, the poet Martial seems to have fondly sipped the juice of leeks quite a bit. He wrote this description of a banquet he was to hold:

My bailiff's wife has brought me mallows to aid digestion, and other treasures of the garden. Among them are lettuces and leeks for slicing; and there is no lack of mint—the antidote to flatulence—and stimulant elecampane.

But, perhaps the most famous leek lover was Nero, the looney emperor who not only fiddled while Rome burned, but who regularly ate leeks to clear his throat and sweeten his speaking voice, thus earning him the nickname "Porrophagus" or "Leek-Eater."

It was the spread of the Roman Empire that brought alliums like garlic throughout Europe and made it a household word in many languages.

HOUSEHOLD WORDS IN MANY LANGUAGES

Onion

English—*onion*
Welsh—*gibbons*
   (*spring onions*)
French—*oignon, ciboule*
   (*spring onion*)
Spanish—*cebolla*
German—*zwiebel*
Italian—*cipolla*
Greek—*krommuon*
Chinese—*yang-ts'ung*
Japanese—*tamanegi*

Arabic—*basal*
Russian—*luk*
Swahili—*kitunguu*
Turkish—*sogan*
Persian—*goondina*
Indian—*piyaz*
Yiddish—*tsibele*
Swedish—*rödlök*
Dutch—*ui*
Portuguese—*cebola*

Garlic

English—*garlic*
Country English—
   poor man's treacle
French—*ail*
Spanish—*ajo*
German—*knoblauch*
Italian—*aglio*

Russian—*chesnok*
Swahili—*kitunguu*
   saumu
Turkish—*sarmisak*
Persian—*sir*
Indian—*lashuna*
Yiddish—*knoble*

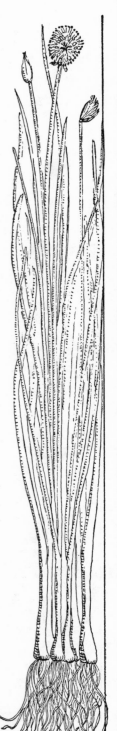

Greek—*skordo*
(*skortho*)
Chinese—*suan*
Japanese—*ninniku*
Arabic—*som or thūm*

Swedish—*vitlök*
Dutch—*knoflook*
Portuguese—*alho*
Malayan—*bayang
putch*

Leek

English—*leek*
French—*poireau,
porreau*
Spanish—*puerro*
German—*lauch, porree*
Italian—*porro*
Greek—*prason*
Chinese—*tsung*
Russian—*luk*

Swahili—*namna
yakitunguu kidogo*
Arabic—*basal*
Persian—*goondina*
Indian—*dungali, kânda,
piyaz*
Swedish—*lök*
Dutch—*look*

Chives

English—*chives*
Country English—
rushleek
French—*ciboulette, cive*
Spanish—*cebollino*
German—*schnittlauch*
Italian—*cipollina,
aglio di serpe*

Portuguese—*cebolinha*
Arabic—*basal*
Russian—*luk-rezanyets*
Chinese—*hsia-ye-
ts'ung*
Japanese—*asatsuki*
Swedish—*gräslök*
Dutch—*bieslook*

You may be interested to know how some of these vegetables got their English names. Well, in Rome, the onion was called *unio* because the bulb is *one*, united, unlike garlic which is split into cloves. The word also means "a pearl," and eventually, *unio* became the name for the little white pearl onions so popular in cocktails. In France, thanks to the Normans and the Gauls and all, the word *unio* became *ognon*, and, by the Middle Ages, *oignon*. From there, it was a short Anglo-Saxon step to *onyon* and, finally, *onion*. Actually, the Romans had three words for onion; the other two, *bulbus* (from the Greek) and *caepa*, also gave English and Italian a couple of words. From *bulbus*, which meant both an onion and a bulbous root, we get *bulb*. And *caepa* (head) gave the world *cipolla*, the modern Italian word for onion. By the way, there is also a theory that onion is a corruption of the word *usnio*, linked to the Sanskrit *ushna*, meaning "burning" or "stinging," just as *allium* came from the Celtic "al" for "burning." However, there seems to be more evidence for the *unio* idea.

As for *leek* and *garlic*, both come from the Hebrew and German (Saxon) words for herb or plant. The Anglo-Saxon word was often spelled *leac;* gardens were called *leac-tuns* and gardeners *leac-wards*. Garlic is derived from the Old Norse

gar (spear) and *leac* (spear-plant) probably because of the shape and way it comes out of the ground. And *chives* come from the French *cive* from the Latin *caepa* or head, while *shallot* is derived from the Old French *eschaloigne* from the Latin Ascalonia, which is now the seaport Ashkelon on the Mediterranean coast of Israel.

Alliums A.D. or Middle-Age Spread

> *Give onyons to Saynt Cutlake*
> *And Garlycke to Saynt Cryryake;*
> *If ye will sun the headake,*
> *Ye shall have them at Queenhyth.*

The above is a cryptic Anglo-Saxon or Celtic charm, indicating that the alliums have influenced not only cooking and sundry, but literature as well. Sadly, they were soon to fall from grace both in cooking and literature. Even as early as the 5th century, Sidonius Apollinaris complained about his large, onion-chewing French masters:

> *Wouldst know what terrifies my Muse,*
> *What is it she complains on?*
> *How can she write a six foot line*
> *With seven feet of patron?*
> *O happy eyes! O happy ears!*
> *Too happy, happy nose,*
> *That smells not onions all day long,*
> *For whom no garlic grows!*

Garlic also gave its name to a contemptuous word for a fellow with a bald head—*pilgarlic*—because his pate looked like a peeled bulb of garlic. The word was also possibly applied to a leper, maybe because of his hair loss and skin condition, or perhaps because garlic was used as a scalp tonic and a treatment for leprosy.

But, basically, as yet garlic and its relatives were treasured. Charlemagne ordered chives grown in his gardens. Via the Crusades, shallots made their grand entrance into European culinary arts. And in Siberia, until the middle of the 18th century, the people paid their taxes in garlic: fifteen bulbs for a man, ten for a woman and five for each child. And elsewhere, alliums were still magical.

In a Medieval Danish tale told by Saxo Grammaticus (whose *Ur Hamlet* was to provide the basis for a famous play of a similar title), the onion even figures in what writer Robert Graves in his book *The White Goddess* calls a *love-test*. Aslog, the last of the Volsungs, was living on a farm in Norway, disguised as a sooty scullery maid named Krake (raven) when Ragnar Lodbrog fell in love with her. As a test of her worthiness, Ragnar told her to come to him "neither on foot nor riding, neither dressed nor naked, neither fasting nor feasting, neither attended nor alone. She arrived on goatback, one foot trailing on the

ground, clothed only in her hair and a fishing-net, holding an onion to her lips, a hound by her side." And she passed the test. Graves says that this legend was to inspire the Lady Godiva story, as well as others. But, minus the onion.

The British have uses for the onion different from the love-test. In the Middle Ages, alliums were cheap and everyone used them—fried, stewed or eaten raw with cheese and bread. There was so much pounding of garlic for sauces, this proverb arose: *"The mortar always smells of garlic."* Even ascetics liked the alliums. Cuthbert, a 7th century English saint, let himself nibble raw onions during his final fast. Unfortunately, he didn't eat enough of them. He died. Other holy men were not so masochistic. In many Medieval monasteries, a favorite dish (which also happens to be full of Vitamin C) was a mixture of chopped onions and chopped violets eaten raw as a savory or cooked in a broth. Another was *Sauce Robert*—onions simmered in butter, then cooked long in broth. And there was also *Sauce Vert*—parsley, mint, dittany, thyme, alecost (the herb cost-mary), garlic, vinegar, pepper, salt and eisel wine (a sour wine product)—which was used on many a dish.

Of all Medieval people, women were not supposed to eat a lot of alliums—particularly garlic—especially when entertaining a sweet-

heart. As Bulleyn wrote of garlic centuries later in his *Book of Simples* (1579):

> It is a grosse kynde of medycine, very unpleasant for fayre ladyes, and tender lilly rose-coloured damselles, which oftentimes preferre sweete breathes before gentle words, but both would do very well.

However, in the Middle Ages, many fayre ladyes still indulged in the grosse herb.

On other continents, the alliums were favorite Medieval fare. The taste for them in China, Korea and the Middle East has already been mentioned. In Africa too alliums were popular. In Sansandi (West Africa), onions were sliced, ground in a wooden mortar, dried and mixed with butter, and formed into balls called *láwashi*, which were eaten with relish!

> *I like the leeke above all herbs and floures;*
> *When first we wore the same, the field was ours,*
> *The leeke is white and green, whereby is meant*
> *That Britaines are both stout and eminente.*
> *Next to the lion and the unicorne*
> *The leeke the fairest emblym that is worn.*
>
> From an ancient manuscript
> in the British Museum

In Medieval Europe, the nation with which an allium was most identified was Wales. The leeks and the Welsh are inextricably bound—

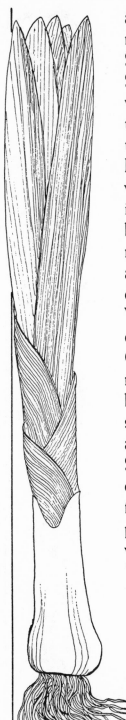

although there are many theories as to why. The most familiar story is that in 640 A.D., when the Saxons invaded Wales, Cadwallader, following St. David's instruction, ordered the Welsh to wear leeks on their caps to distinguish them from the enemy. The Welsh won the battle, and, to this day, celebrate their victory on March 1, St. David's Day, the Day of the Leek, by wearing the vegetable. Some historians claim that St. David's idea came from the fact that long before this battle, the Welsh used to gather leeks from nearby gardens and wear them in their hats to avoid mistaken identity and accidents from their own men. Others say that before plowing land, Welsh farmers shared a common meal to which each contributed a leek. And herbalist Rosetta Clarkson feels the wearing of the leek on March 1 might have begun because that's when farming began in earnest. At any rate, by the Renaissance, the Welsh were stuck with this emblem, and they and leeks could not be separated. In Shakespeare's *Henry V*, Pistol ridicules the custom of wearing this allium and is then forced by the fiery Welshman Fluellen to "eat the leek," a phrase which had come to mean "to eat one's words." And, in his book, Rev. Friend quotes:

> *March, various, fierce, and wild with wind-crackt cheeks,*

By wilder Welshmen led, and crown'd with Leeks.

Besides being the herb for March 1, the leek is also listed as the birthday plant for February 9, and it supposedly signifies courage and liveliness.

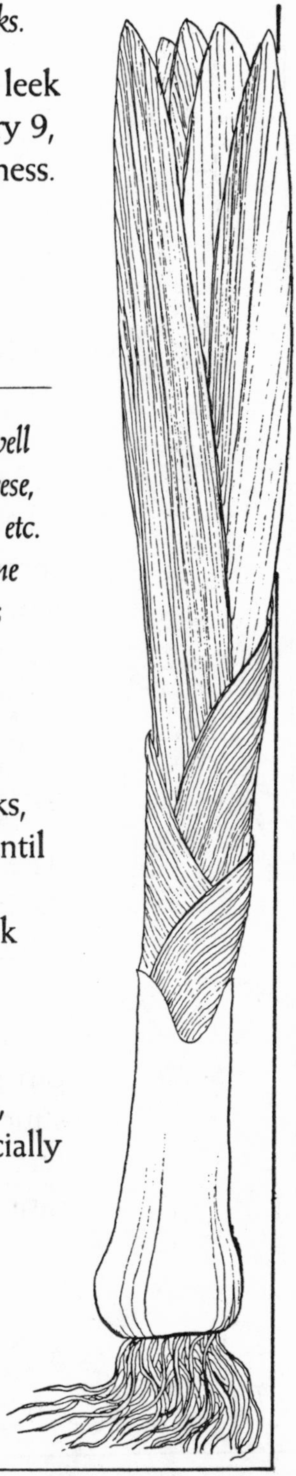

Howard and Rosemary's Leeks in Vinegar (written by Howard Roberts)

Leeks
Pepper
Coriander seed, ground if dried; soft and whole are better
A few onion rings
Anything that goes well with leeks: e.g. cheese, tomato, capsicum, etc.
Vinegar (German wine vinegar with herbs is best)

This recipe has been extensively extemporized—so if it tastes good with leeks, sling it in! Whatever it is. Cook the leeks until soft. Drain well. Allow to grow cold and marinate in vinegar with coriander and black pepper added. If seeds are soft enough to chew, poke them between the leaves of the leek. Garnish with the onion rings and anything available—tomato, pepper, cheese, etc. Goes well with almost any salad, especially smoked mackerel.

58

Leeks and Ham
Another leek recipe from Howard and
Rosemary—(written by Howard Roberts)

3-4 slices smoked ham
  (possibly even
  pastrami)
Leeks
	Cheese sauce
	Grated cheese, paprika,
	  pepper
	Tomato

Parboil the leeks (don't cook them too much).
Allow to cool off and wrap in ham. Lay in a
flat oven-proof dish. Make up cheese sauce
until *very* thick. Spread over leeks. Sprinkle
with grated cheese, paprika, pepper and sliced
tomato. Bake in a moderate oven until the top
is browned. Very good with spinach and fried
courgettes (*zucchini*).

A PLAGUE ON BOTH YOUR HOUSES

The Middle Ages were not an easy time to live.
Besides things like the Inquisition and the
Crusades, there were also numerous bouts of the
plague. And the alliums—especially garlic—were
thought to be (and probably were) powerful
protection against the pestilence. Garlic was
strung from doorways, roof beams, bed posts. It
was stuffed in cellars, worn as necklaces. A
disinfectant called "Four Thieves Vinegar" was

supposed to have been used by four crooks who stole valuables from persons dead of the disease. The ingredients: Beach and Roman wormwood, rosemary, sage, mint, rue, lavender flowers, calamus powder, cinnamon, cloves, nutmeg and plenty of *garlic*, mixed with red wine, and, later, after distillation and filtration, camphor. The stuff might also have been named after Richard Forhaves, who reputedly sold it. At any rate, it was certainly a popular potion. In heavy garlic-eating countries such as France, the incidence of plague among priests who tended to the sick was much less than in places like Great Britain, where they didn't munch a bunch. Two seventeenth century writers, Samuel Pepys in his diaries and Daniel Defoe in his *Journal of the Plague Year* (the Middle Ages were not the only times the plague struck) wrote of a fortunately healthy family whose home, called GOD'S PROVIDENT HOUSE, had vast stores of garlic in the kitchen and the cellar.

Garlic worn as a necklace will stop your soul from leaving your body.

In many parts of Europe, notably Eastern Europe and the Balkan countries, people thought that diseases like the plague were caused by evil spirits, especially VAMPIRES. If garlic could

ward off other horrible creatures, it could do the same for vampires, the people thought. And anybody who has ever read or seen a film version of Bram Stoker's *Dracula* knows they were right. A necklace of garlic and garlic at the windows and door will keep the blood-sucker away. However, if the vampire has already struck, it might be necessary to take more severe measures.

How to Kill a Vampire

At dawn, or later in the day, go to the vampire's castle (or more modest home). Find his/her coffin. Open the lid. Scatter garlic over the undead. Take a pointed stake and drive it through the fiend's heart. Ignore the groans and screams and keep driving in that stake until the vampire is truly dead. Then, cut off the corpse's head. Burn it and the body to ashes.

An Anglo-Saxon Riddle

I was alive and said nothing; even so I die.
Back I came before I was. Everyone plunders me,
Keeps me confined and shears my head,
Bites my bare body, breaks my sprouts.
No man I bite unless he bites me;
Many there are who do bite me.

Answer: An onion or a leek, of course!

Many there were in the Renaissance who did bite the allium. Lord Bacon had his onion

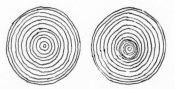

fields bordered with chives. Sixteenth century Parisians mixed garlic with butter every spring and ate loads of it for health and for fun (a practice still followed today in parts of France). And when the French king Henri IV was born at Pau in 1553, his lips were rubbed with garlic and red wine, a local Béarnais tradition to make him hearty. This act must have worked for not only was Henri hearty, but a great gourmet as well.

To Butter Onions

Take apples and onions, mince the onions and slice the apples. Put them in a pot, but more apple than onions, and bake them with the household bread. Close up the pot with paste or paper; when you use them, butter them with butter, sugar and boild currans, serve them on sippets, and scrape on sugar and cinnamon.

Robert May, *The Accomplisht Cook*

Apples and Onions
A More Modern Version

2-3 *large Spanish onions, sliced*
3 *large cooking apples, sliced*

2 *tablespoons brown sugar*
½ *cup water*
Butter for cooking
Salt to taste

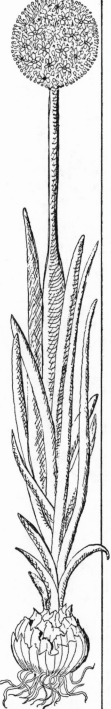

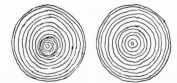

Cook the sliced onions in butter until nearly soft. Add the sliced apples to the onions. Pour in the water and sprinkle with salt. Cover and cook for about 15 minutes at moderate heat until the apples are soft but not mushy. Uncover, sprinkle with brown sugar and turn up the heat to reduce any extra water. Serves 4.

The Elizabethans were divided on the issue of alliums. The herbalist Thomas Tusser thought leeks a tasty vegetable. In his 500 *Points of Good Husbandry*, he wrote:

> *Now leeks are in season, for pottage full good,*
> *And spareth the milch-cow, and purgeth the blood:*
> *These having with peason, for pottage in Lent,*
> *Thou sparest both oatmeal and bread to be spent.*

Others must have agreed with him for leek recipes such as the following were popular:

A Sallet of Boyled Leeks

Parboyle leeks and chop them fine with the edges of two hard Trenchers upon a board, or the backs of two Chopping-knives; then set them on a Chafing dish of coales with Butter and Vinegar. Season it with Sinamon, Ginger, Sugar, and a few parboyled Currans. Then cut

hard Egges into quarters to garnish it withall and serve it upon Sippets. Egges are necessary, or at least very good for all boyled Sallets.

John Murrell, *A New Booke of Cookerie*

Just as popular were onion recipes like the abovementioned "To Butter Onions" and Gervase Markham's "To Prepare Chibols, or Scallions" from *The English Huswife*:

Chibols pilled [Welsh onions peeled], washt clean, and half the green topps cut clean away, so served on a fruit dish; or ... scallions ... which such like serve up simply.

Markham, and other allium enthusiasts, felt that raw green onions were a good way to begin a meal as they were appetite stimulants. But some of them also felt that onions caused weight loss—something not appreciated by those appreciators of the plump, the Elizabethans. Onion lovers also felt the vegetable was good for over-drinking and insomnia. And, as Dr. Andrewe Boorde said, "They (onions)... putteth away fastydyousness," which he thought was a good thing to putteth away. Garlic too had its champions like Thomas Hyll, who wrote in *A Most Brief and Pleasaunt Treatise Teachyng How to Dresse, Sow and Set a Garden*

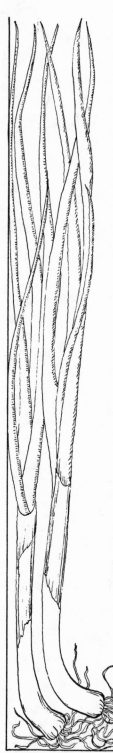

64

(circa 1558), the first English book on gardening, "And eating it also, a man may the safelyer go after by stinckyng places because ye stronge savour of it doth overcome all other savours and stinckes."

Although there were many English allium-fans, there were also many who loathed these foods, probably because the French, Spanish and Italians ate them. Alliums "engendered choler" and made a person oversexed, they said. The smell was crude, vulgar, they said, a sign of lowness. A beggar, in Shakespeare's words, would mouth "brown bread and garlic." Garlic, above all, was treated with hostility. John Evelyn, a colonial American of British descent, in his *Acetaria, a Discourse of Sallets* (1699), wrote favorably of other alliums:

The best (onions) are such as are brought us out of *Spain*, and some that have weighed eight Pounds. Choose therefore the large, sound, white, and thin Skinned. Being eaten crude and alone with Oil, Vinegar, and Pepper, we use them in Sallet, not so hot as Garlic, nor at all so rank. In *Italy* they frequently make a *Sallet* of *Scallions*, *Chives*, and *Chibols* only seasoned with Oil and Pepper; and an honest laborious Country-man, with good *Bread*, Salt, and a little Parsley, will make a contented Meal with a roasted Onion.

But, when it came to speaking of garlic, Evelyn said:

> ... we absolutely forbid it entrance into our Salleting, by reason of its intolerable rankness, and which made it so detested of old that the eating of it was (as we read) part of the Punishment for such as had committed the horrid'st Crimes.

And Thomas Nashe, an English satirist, summed up alliaversion[1] neatly: "Garlick maketh a man wyncke, drynke and stynke." (Translation—"Garlic makes a man wink, drink and stink.")[2]

However, allium-hatred was not confined to the British, as you're about to see. Alliaversion spread all over Europe, even to France, until the early nineteenth century and the emergence of *haute cuisine* or Hotsy-Totsy Cooking, which made garlic more than respectable.

[1] Alliaversion—aversion to (hatred of) alliums.

[2] A Garlic champion, Sir John Harington, disputed Nashe's lines (and incorporated some of Robert of Normandy's) in this poem on the Salerno medical school (1609):
Six things, that here in order shall ensue,
Against all poisons have a secret power,
Pear, Garlic, Radish-roots, Nuts, Rape and Rue.
But *Garlic* chief. For they that it devour,
May drink, and care not who their drink do brew;
May walk in airs infected every hour.
Since *Garlic* then hath powers to save from death,
Bear with it though it make unsavoury breath,
And scorn not Garlic, like to some that think
It only makes men wink, and drink, and stink!

GREAT ALLIUM-HATERS OF THE WORLD

1. Horace, Roman poet. He got sick after a heavy meal and blamed it on the garlic which he called "more poisonous than Hemlock."

2. Chaucer, English poet. He describes his lusty, greedy, syphilis-ridden Summoner: "Garlic he loved, and onions too, and leeks/And drinking strong red wine till all was hazy."

3. The Spanish Queen Isabel the Catholic, who not only detested the smell of garlic, but who wouldn't eat parsley because it grew near garlic! She said, "Disimulado venía el villano vestido de verde." ("The base fellow came disguised in green.")

4. The Spanish King Alfonso XI, who hated garlic so much that in 1330 he founded a knightly order based on this hatred. A knight who had eaten it could not appear in court or communicate with other knights for at least a month.

5. The Author's friend Andrew Ramer,

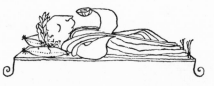

who said, "When I eat garlic, my tongue becomes numb."

6.   William Bowyer, of whom Samuel Pepys writes:

And so home, and thither came with Bowyer and dined with us; but strange to see how he could not endure onyons in sauce to lamb, but was overcome with the sight of it, and so was forced to make his dinner of an egg or two.

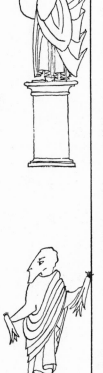

7.   Hoosiers from Gary, Indiana. A law on the books there states: "It is illegal to take a streetcar or go to the theater within four hours of consuming garlic."

8.   Peter Sourdain, professor of English, who went to court to stop a French restaurant, La Goulue, from "emitting nuisances." He lost. The judge ruled that those were not nuisances but the "redolent odors of garlic... the wafted odors of sauces and stews."

9.   Ana Lucia Agudelo, Colombian Miss Universe contestant, who said that the European entrants "smelled very bad. Even the prettiest women in Europe smell of garlic and onion."

10.   Americans. In a survey by L.M. Boyd

in *The San Francisco Chronicle*, Americans said that the odors they hate most are: 1) Garlic; 2) Lard; 3) Olive Oil. (Best-liked smells: hot coffee, strawberries and apples).

This aversion to alliums seems to have even carried over to dreams and superstitions. The English *Royal Dream Book* says to dream of garlic indicates the discovery of hidden treasures, but also the approach of some domestic quarrel. Richard Folkard writes:

> *To dream of eating onions means*
> *Much strife in thy domestic scenes,*
> *Secrets found out or else betrayed,*
> *And many falsehoods made and said.*

And in the Ozarks, onion peel is always burned or bad financial luck will result.

Fortunately, some of this hatred of alliums has disappeared. After all, nowadays, who hasn't heard of garlic bread or onions on pizza? You haven't? Well, then, here are two recipes:

Garlic Bread

1 stale loaf of bread
Olive oil or butter

5 cloves garlic, minced finely

Split bread lengthwise. Spread with oil or butter. Sprinkle on garlic. Put halves together. Wrap in aluminum foil. Bake at 350° for ½ hour.

Steve's Matzoh Pizzas

4 matzohs
3 cups canned Italian
    tomatoes, drained
    and chopped
1 teaspoon oregano

½ pound mozzarella
    cheese, shredded
2 onions, sliced
Olive oil

Put the tomatoes on the matzohs. Sprinkle with oregano. Spread on the mozzarella and onions. Sprinkle with olive oil. Bake in a hot oven until the cheese is brown. Serves 4.

However, even now, England and the other British Isles are still the bastion of alliaversion where onions and leeks (and rarely garlic) are used in cooking (but not raw) and still made fun of.

Come, follow me by the smell,
Here are delicate onyons to sell;
I promise to use you well.
They make the blood warmer,
You'll feed like a farmer;

For this is every cook's opinion,
No savoury dish without an onyon;
But, lest your kissing should be spoiled,
Your onyons must be thoroughly boiled:
Or else you may spare
Your mistress a share,
The secret will never be known:
She cannot discover
The breath of her lover,
But think it as sweet as her own.

Jonathan Swift, *Onyons*, 1746

TWO POST-RENAISSANCE DEFINITIONS AND AN EXPENSIVE MISTAKE

Onion

Thieves' slang for a seal or the like worn on a watch-chain. *"With my fawnied famms, and my onions gay."* William H. Ainsworth, *Rookwood* (Translation—"With my ringed hands, and my seals gay.")

Garlic

The name of a popular dance of the early seventeenth century.

"And for his action he eclipseth quite,
The Jig of 'Garlick,' and the 'Punk's Delight.'"

Taylor, the Water-poet, 1615

Three hundred years ago, a sailor delivered

some goods to a Dutch businessman, and was then invited to have breakfast. The sailor reached for what he thought was an onion and ate it with his smoked herring. He claimed it wasn't a very tasty onion, but he ate it just the same. Imagine the horror of the businessman (and the sailor, who landed in the brig for awhile) when he discovered that the seafarer had munched a tulip bulb *(Semper Augustus)* worth $1,500!

Garlic Black Beans and Rice

3 tablespoons olive oil
3 cloves garlic,
  chopped fine

¼ teaspoon cumin
1 can black beans

Fry the garlic in the oil until just brown. Sprinkle in the cumin. Stir. Mix in the black beans. Serve on rice. Serves 4.

While overpriced tulips were coming to Holland, the cultivated onion and its relatives arrived in the Americas. The first mention of *Allium sativum* (garlic, remember?) in America seems to be that Cortes ate it in 16th century Mexico, although Columbus may also have introduced it a few years earlier. An old Spanish proverb, "Ajo puro y vino crudo, passar el puerto seguro" ("Pure garlic and crude wine to cross the

mountain pass safely") seems to have been taken seriously by Cortes and later by the early nineteenth century revolutionaries San Martín and O'Higgins who, when they crossed the Andes, put garlic into the nostrils of their horses and mules that collapsed from lack of oxygen (our northern neighbors, the Canadians, also gave garlic to their horses for endurance on long prairie runs). It was the Spanish too who probably brought the onion to South America via the West Indies. Other European settlers—and conquerors—brought chives and onions to North America, to be used once again in cooking, medicine and the making of jokes like that Father of Proverbs Ben Franklin's "Onions can make even heirs and widows weep."

ALLIUM APHORISMS
(Proverbs, Phrases and Such)

1. Spruce as an onion.
2. To know one's onions.
3. To weep with the onion.
4. Green as a leek (Shakespeare even wrote in *A Midsummer Night's Dream,* "His eyes were green as leeks.").
5. Not worth a leek.

And two Yiddish curses:
Zol dir vaksn tsibeles fun pupik!
(Onions should grow from your navel!)

Zolst vaksn vi a tsibele mit der kop in drerd!
(You should grow like an onion with your head in
the ground!)

Although cultivated alliums were not
brought to the Americas until the sixteenth and
seventeenth centuries, wild alliums were certainly
around long before them. Native Americans used
them in every conceivable way— boiled, roasted,
sauteed, raw, in syrups, as poultices, for dyes and
even toys. During his stay at Fort Clark, Prince
Maximilian, near death from scurvy (a disease
caused by the lack of Vitamin C), was saved by a
Black cook and Dakota Sioux children who fed
him wild onions full of Vitamin C. And the
Illinois Indians who saved Father Marquette and
his crew from starvation in Illinois by feeding
them wild garlic named the spot CicagaWunj—
Place of Wild Garlic. That name, that place
became Chicago.

OTHER SPOTS NAMED FOR ALLIUMS
1. Onion River, Vermont—so named
   because wild onions grew on its banks.
2. L'Oignon, Burgundy—so named

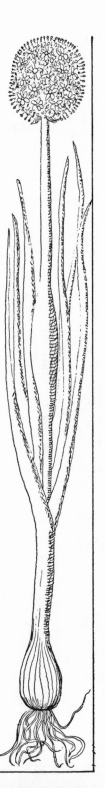

because wild onions grew on its banks.

3. Onion Mountain Chain, Turkestan— so named because wild onions grew all over it.

Speaking of scurvy (and we were, a few lines back), Native Americans were not the only people who knew of the anti-scorbutic (anti-scurvy) function of alliums. The onion has long been a staple item for sailors. One English captain insisted that each member of his crew eat an onion a day. The Captain might have been unpopular with his men, but his rule prevented them from getting scurvy. And in Australia, prospectors and gold miners also used onions, the only vegetables that could be stored for long periods in a hot climate, to prevent this disease.

Grapefruit and Onion Salad
(A Delicious Anti-Scorbutic)

2 fresh grapefruits   *1 can black olives*
1 large Spanish onion

Peel and section the grapefruit. Slice the onion into rings. Drain the olives. Mix the whole batch together and toss gently with vinaigrette dressing. Serves 4.

Vinaigrette Dressing

¼ cup olive oil
1 tablespoon vinegar

¼ teaspoon prepared
mustard
Salt and pepper

Blend the ingredients and serve. For green salads, a clove of garlic should first be rubbed around the bowl.

Now back to America. In the U.S., the "rose of roots," as R.L. Stevenson called the onion, has been used for other healthful properties—in particular, its antiseptic ones. During the Civil War, General Grant, who used onion juice to clean wounds, sent a memo to the War Department which read, "I will not move my troops without onions." He was quickly sent three cartloads. In World War I, too, garlic juice was dripped into sphagnum moss and wrapped about wounds.

Onions have also been used in America to predict weather.

TRUE OR FALSE QUIZ

Onion's skin very thin,
Mild winter's coming in;
Onion's skin thick and tough

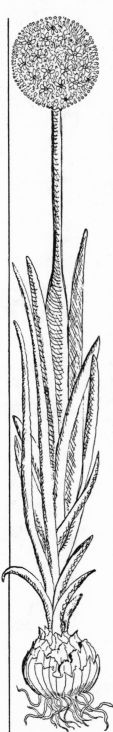

Coming winter cold and rough.
Answer: Possibly true.

On New Year's Day, cut six onions in half. Scoop out the inner layers of each and place salt in the twelve halves, one for each month of the year. After twelve days, the onions in which the salt has dissolved will be the wet months to come.
Answer: No dice.

AN AMERICAN TALL TALE
(based on information from John Harris)

Everybody knows here in the Southwest there grows a Giant Garlic. Some say that the avalanche at Possum Creek was caused by it. Others claim the collapse of the Carter Mine had something to do with a loose clove or two. But them's just rumors. Now if you really want to know the truth, it's this. You remember that head-on collision a few months back between the Sunshine Special and the Gold Dust Locomotive? Well, I know for a fact Mr. Morton weren't too pleased with Mr. Jones' Gold Dust, his chief competition. And I hear tell he was seen talking to some ruffians hereabouts. And Mr. Jones, well, he weren't too de-lighted by Mr. Morton's Sunshine Special. And one day, he went up to this other bunch of hooligans. And then came Cross Mile Day, and that test run. Well, Mr. Morton's boys pulled one switch, and Mr. Jones' boys pulled another. And before

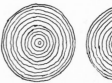

you could say "Chili Con Carne!" them trains just crashed. Funny thing, though. Nobody knows who trucked out that durn Garlic. Some folks think it just took it into its own head to roll onto the tracks. Course I think that's a bit crazy, if you ask me. Anyway, it don't really matter. What did is that it took a week to haul that Garlic out of there. Wouldn't you just know that thing came from Texas? We grow everything bigger here!

ALLIUM ECONOMY
or
What's all of this got to do with the price of onions?

Onion Producers of the World

In the Middle Ages, Flanders produced most of Europe's onions. At the present time (or, at least, as of 1976), the leading onion exporter is Holland—followed by Spain, the U.S. and Egypt. Other top exporters are India, Italy, and Bermuda (where Bermudans are nicknamed—what else—*onions*).

In the U.S., the onion holds fourth place among the commercial vegetable crops. About fifteen million bushels are raised annually. California and Texas are the top producers. Onions

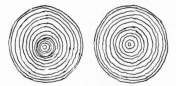

are imported by the U.S. from Southern Europe, Bermuda and the West Indies.

Garlic Producers of the World

In 1969, garlic growers in the Western U.S. produced eighty-four million pounds of garlic. Presently, the U.S. produces about fifty-eight thousand short tons of garlic a year—almost twenty percent more than ten years ago!

Arleux, a French village north of Paris, claims to be the garlic capital of the world, having about three thousand garlic growers. According to Arleux's mayor, in 1977 the town produced more than two million pounds of garlic, allowing for all of France's needs and even exportation!

Two garlic capitals of the U.S.A.:

Gilroy, California—for production

New York City, N.Y.—for consumption

After all, what other city besides New York could have produced the following Yiddish slogan:

Three nickles vill get ya on the subway,

But knoble [garlic] vill get ya a seat.

ALLIUMS IN THE ARTS

In the visual arts, onions and other alliums have been much depicted. Giuseppe Arcimboldo, offi-

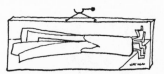

cial portrait painter to Maximilian II, sixteenth century king of Bohemia, and to his successor, Rudolph II, created bizarre heads with garlic cheeks, corn cob ears and scallion lobes. Seventeenth century still-life paintings especially showed rich tables overflowing with onions and other food, an indication of great wealth. And one of Cézanne's famous works shows a luscious array of red onions.

And let us not forget that artists cook creatively, too.

Susan Dallas' Chili (Guaranteed to Make You See The Light)

½ pound suet
4 pounds ground beef
  (coarse venison or,
  best, chopped chuck)
¾ teaspoon paprika
1½ tablespoons chili
  powder
½ tablespoon cumin
1 tablespoon salt

1 teaspoon cayenne
  pepper
1½ tablespoons chili
  peppers, finely diced
3 or more cloves garlic
3 cups water
2 small cans tomato
  sauce (optional)

Fry suet in a heavy Dutch oven. Add the meat and other ingredients and 1½ cups water. Cook slowly for 1 hour or until the meat is done. Add the remaining water. Simmer 1 hour

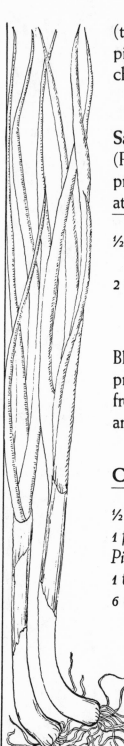

(tomatos are added here). Serve with Texas pintos, cumin rice, fresh red onions and strong cheddar cheese.

Sari Dienes' Creamed Spinach With Yogurt
(Published for the occasion of her performance presentation at the Fourth S.E.M. Spring Festival at the Albright-Knox Art Gallery, Buffalo, N.Y.)

½ pound Spinach,
   coarsely chopped
2 tablespoons Safflower,
   or other light oil,
   added very slowly

½ cup Yogurt
2 Cloves Garlic, chopped
3 Grapefruit sections,
   unpeeled

Blend together on medium speed. Spinach produces a brilliant bright green, quite different from the olive color of the dandelion [from another recipe]. Yield—1½ cups.

Carolee Schneemann's Family Fiesta Fish

½ pound shrimps
1 pound mussels
Pinch of red pepper
1 tablespoon olive oil
6 cloves garlic, chopped
   medium fine

½ pound sea scallops
1 pound whiting or
   haddock filet
1 tablespoon sherry
Juice of 1 whole lemon
Ground pepper

1 tablespoon tamari sauce   4 leaves of seaweed
1 bunch scallions   (wakame, dulse, etc.)

Steam the shrimp and mussels in water with the red pepper until the mussels just open and the shrimp just turns pink. Rinse the shrimp under water and let the mussels cool. Shell and devein the shrimp. Remove the mussels from their shells. Take a heavy saucepan and put in the oil. Heat and add the garlic. Stir. Add the tamari and scallions. Then, put in the scallops and the fish, cubed. Add the shrimp, mussels and the rest of the ingredients. Stir. When the mixture is steamy, turn the heat off. Cover with a lid. In a minute, the dish will be done. Serve with spinach noodles and sour cream cheese dressing. Serves 6.

In ceramics and architecture onions have also been influential. A set of Delft ware in the famous Meissen blue onion design was once a status symbol in Germany. Today, this antique china is quite valuable. And onion domes are found all over the world on Eastern Orthodox churches. The Cathedral of the Assumption in Moscow has five of them!

The allium, like the bean, is truly a musical fruit (the more you eat, the more you toot. The

more you toot, the better you feel, so eat 'em both at every meal!). In the opera *Le Jongleur de Notre Dame* (*Our Lady's Juggler*), the baritone peels a leek while singing "Legend of the Sagebrush." The Incredible String Band named their first album "5,000 Spirits, or the Layers of the Onion." Booker T and the MG's recorded the famous "Green Onions." And the Author has written a wonderful tune with this title and lyrics:

I've Got Tears in My Eyes, Though I Ain't Been Eating Onions, 'Cause My Honey Lamb Has Left Me in a Stew

Oh, I wish I had an onion
To rub upon the bunion
In my heart.

Well, my sweetie used to love me,
Used to turtle-dove me,
But just like cloves of garlic
We fell apart.

Oh, I wish I had some chives
To wipe out all the hives
In my mind.

For my cookie used to kiss me,
And tell me that he'd miss me,
But like folks who stomp on shallots,
He was unkind.

Oh, I would sail a galleon,
Loaded up with scallion
On the sea.

If my sugar pie would come home,
So I won't be alone,
Just like a long, lonely leek
In a tall tree.

In the area of film, Les Blank, well-known for his documentaries on regional cultures—especially their music and food—has completed *Garlic Is As Good As Ten Mothers*, a movie about garlic. The film features John Harris, herbalist Jeanne Rose and a garlic feast held on Bastille Day, July 14, 1976, at Chez Panisse in Berkeley, California. The menu for this gala consisted of:

Whole Garlics and Mushrooms
Baked Chicken Legs with Garlic Puree
Garlic Mayonnaise with Green Beans and
 Potatoes
Fresh Pasta with Sauce Pistou (Basil and
 Garlic Sauce)
Beef Tripe with Basil and Garlic
Poached Fish with Aioli (Bourride)
Leg of Lamb with Garlic Marinade
Pureed Potatoes with Garlic Cream
Garlic Ice Cream Sundae LSR (Lovers of
 the Stinking Rose)

84

Here's the ice cream recipe from *Garlic Times*:

Garlic Ice Cream Sundae LSR

At least two weeks, but preferably one month prior to your garlic feast, place ten whole peeled cloves of garlic into one pint of honey. You can also add chopped dates, raisins and chopped, unsalted nuts (almonds, cashews, etc.).

Seal jar and set aside at room temperature.

Every few days, turn jar upside down and leave for several more days. This lets garlic and other ingredients mix with honey, as the dry ingredients tend to rise to the top. (Allow about ¼" between level of honey and lid.)

Taste honey the morning before the feast. It should have a very subtle garlic flavor and bouquet. If too strong, add more honey. If too weak, press a few cloves of garlic through a garlic press and mix thoroughly through the honey. This is best done by placing the jar of honey in a warm water bath until honey liquifies slightly.

Repeat this process of liquifying honey prior to serving.

Scoop balls of vanilla or other light flavored ice cream into dishes and spoon honey over the top. Honey should be warm and slightly liquid to enhance bouquet and eatability. Serves 4.

Blank has also been staging the Smell-Around during screenings of *Always for Pleasure*, his view of the New Orleans Mardi Gras. He and assistants place pots of garlicky red beans and rice around the theatre and fan the odor to the audience. Blank writes, "Red Beans and Rice is what all kinds of people in New Orleans eat on Monday nights and many festive occasions. It's inexpensive, easy to make, goes a long way, keeps a long time, can be frozen, smells great when cooking, tastes fantastic, and is very good for you."

Red Beans and Rice

2 cups dried red beans
7 cups water
1 pound smoked ham
   hocks
2 chopped onions
1 chopped bell pepper
2 chopped ribs celery

1 chopped head fresh
   garlic
3 bay leaves
1½ teaspoons cayenne
Black pepper to taste
Parsley and green onions

Soak beans in water overnight. Add meat, bring to boil, lower to simmer for 1½ hours. Add the rest except the garlic, the parsley and the

onions, and simmer for 1⅓ hours until meat falls apart. Add the garlic ten minutes before removing from the heat. Serve over rice and sprinkle with finely chopped parsley and green onions. Goes good with garlic toast or corn bread and crunchy green salad with lots of garlic. For vegetarians, omit the meat and add lots of basil, thyme and oregano.

For further information on Les Blank's films, write to him: c/o Flower Films, 10341 San Pablo Ave., El Cerrito, Ca. 94530.

To join LOVERS OF THE STINKING ROSE, write to: Lovers of the Stinking Rose, 526 Santa Barbara Rd., Berkeley, Ca. 94707.

> *Davyd of Wales loveth well lekes*
> *That will make Gregory lean chekes;*
> *If Edwarde do eate some with them.*
> *Mary sende him to Bedlam.*
>
> *Salysburye Prymer,* 1533

Alliums are mentioned or discussed in so many works of literature by so many authors, it would be impossible to present all of them. Aristophanes, Plutarch, Rabelais, Chaucer, Shakespeare, Cervantes, Dryden, Dumas, Ibsen—the list goes on and on. Ford Madox Ford devotes a portion of *Provence* to garlic and a young woman who loved it so she was ostracized by everyone until "she had schooled her organs to

assimilate, not protest against it, the sacred herb."
And Lawrence Durrell wrote a short story called
"If Garlic Be the Food of Love."

Charles Dudley Warner wrote in *My
Summer in a Garden* (1871).

I am quite ashamed to take friends into my
garden and have them notice the absence of
onions. It is very marked. In onion is strength;
and a garden without it lacks flavor. The onion
in its satin wrappings is among the most
beautiful of vegetables; and it is the only one
that represents the essence of things. It can
almost be said to have a soul. You take off coat
after coat, and the onion is still there; and,
when the last one is removed, who dare say that
the onion itself is destroyed, though, you can
weep over its departed spirit? If there is any one
thing on this fallen earth that the angels in
heaven weep over more than another, it is the
onion.

I know that there is supposed to be a
prejudice against the onion; but I think there is
rather a cowardice in regard to it. I doubt not
that all men and women really love the onion;
but few confess their love. Affection for it is
concealed. Good New Englanders are as shy of
owning it as they are of talking about religion.
Some people have days on which they eat
onions—what you might call "retreats" or their
"Thursdays." The act is the nature of a mystic
ceremony, an Eleusinian mystery: not a breath

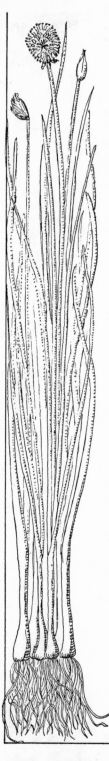

of it must get abroad. On that day, they see no company; they deny the kiss of greeting to the dearest friend; they retire within themselves, and hold communion with one of the most pungent and penetrating manifestations of the moral vegetable world. Happy is said to be the family which can eat onions together. They are, for the time being, separate from the world, and have a harmony of aspiration. There is a hint here for the reformers. Let them become apostles of the onion; let them eat and preach it to their fellows, and circulate tracts of it in the form of seeds. In the onion is the hope of universal brotherhood. If all men will eat onions at all times, they will come into a universal sympathy.

If garlic abounds in literature, onions seem even more prevalent and symbolic, as the above quote indicates. In *Peer Gynt*, the onion is a tragic-comic symbol of the hero's life's emptiness. And in Carlos Castenada's *The Second Ring of Power*, the sorcerer La Gorda explains that human beings are made up of "layers of luminosity. . . like an onion." Perhaps this common use of onion as a symbol is because the onion is found in every culture, and so is understood by every culture. The onion is like the sun or the moon. Carl Jung must have appreciated its archetypal value in our collective unconscious.

Western Mono Indians tell a story about six wives who loved to eat wild onions. Their mountain lion hunter husbands, disgusted by the smell of their wives' breaths, made the women sleep outside. This happened three times. Finally, the women decided they'd rather give up their husbands than their onions, so they went up to the mountain where the onions grew and used their eagle-down ropes to float up into the sky. Their husbands grew lonesome and soon used their own magic ropes to float up. But the wives preferred to remain alone and they wouldn't let their husbands catch them. To this day, the men float below the women—as stars! The higher group are the Pleiades, which the Mono call the Young Women; the lower set of stars form the constellation Taurus, or the Young Men.

Here are two of the Author's favorite onion works:

From *The Tin Drum* by Gunter Grass.[1]

The Onion Cellar—and here we see the note of authenticity essential to a successful night club—was a real cellar; in fact, it was quite damp and chilly under foot...

1 From *The Tin Drum*, by Gunter Grass, translated by Ralph Manheim. Copyright © 1961, 1962 by Pantheon Books, a Division of Random House, Inc. Reprinted by permission of Pantheon Books, a Division of Random House, Inc.

The customers were uncomfortably seated on common crates covered with onion sacks, yet the plank tables, scrubbed and spotless, recalled the guests from the mine to a peaceful peasant inn such as we sometimes see in the movies.

That was all! But what about the bar? No bar. Waiter, the menu please! Neither waiter nor menu. In fact, there was no one else but ourselves, the Rhine River Three. Klepp, Scholle, and Oskar sat beneath the staircase that was really a companionway. We arrived at nine, unpacked our instruments, and began to play at about ten. But for the present it is only a quarter past nine and I won't be able to speak about us until later. Right now let us keep an eye on Schmuh, who occasionally shot sparrows with a small-calibre rifle.

As soon as the Onion Cellar had filled up—half-full was regarded as full—Schmuh, the host, donned his shawl. This shawl had been specially made for him. It was cobalt-blue silk, printed with a golden-yellow pattern. I mention all this because the donning of the shawl was significant. The pattern printed on the shawl was made up of golden-yellow onions. The Onion Cellar was not really "open" until Schmuh had put on his shawl.

The customers—businessmen, doctors, lawyers, artists, journalists, theatre and movie people, well-known figures from the sporting world, officials in the provincial and municipal

government, in short, a cross section of the
world which nowadays calls itself intellectual—
came with wives, mistresses, secretaries, interior
decorators, and occasional male mistresses, to
sit on crates covered with burlap. Until Schmuh
put on his golden-yellow onions, the
conversation was subdued, forced, dispirited.
These people wanted to talk, to unburden
themselves, but they couldn't seem to get
started; despite all their efforts, they left the
essential unsaid, talked around it. Yet how eager
they were to spill their guts, to talk from their
hearts, their bowels, their entrails, to forget
about their brains just this once, to lay bare the
raw, unvarnished truth, the man within... if
you'll forgive Oskar a crude metaphor, it was
like laying eggs; you push and push...

The pushing in the Onion Cellar brought
meagre results until Schmuh appeared in his
special shawl. Having been welcomed with a
joyful "Ah!" for which he thanked his kind
guests, he vanished for a few minutes behind a
curtain at the end of the Onion Cellar, where
the toilets and store-room were situated.

But why did a still more joyous "Ah," an
"Ah" of relief and release, welcome the host on
his reappearance? The proprietor of a successful
nightclub disappears behind a curtain, takes
something from the store-room, flings a choice
selection of insults in an undertone at the
washroom attendant who is sitting there reading
an illustrated weekly, reappears in front of the

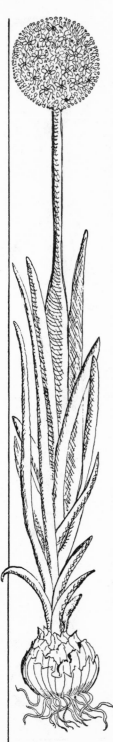

curtain, and is welcomed like the Saviour, like the legendary uncle from Australia!

Schmuh came back with a little basket on his arm and moved among the guests. The basket was covered with a blue-and-yellow checkered napkin. On the cloth lay a considerable number of little wooden boards, shaped like pigs or fish. These he handed out to his guests with little bows and compliments which showed, beyond the shadow of a doubt, that he had grown up in Budapest and Vienna; Schmuh's smile was like the smile on a copy of a copy of the supposedly authentic Mona Lisa.

The guests, however, looked very serious as they took their little boards. Some exchanged boards with their neighbours, for some preferred the silhouette of a pig, while others preferred the more mysterious fish. They sniffed at the pieces of wood and moved them about. Schmuh, after serving the customers in the gallery, waited until all the little boards had come to rest.

Then—and every heart was waiting—he removed the napkin, very much in the manner of a magician: beneath it lay still another napkin, upon which, almost unrecognizable at first glance, lay the paring knives.

These too he proceeded to hand out. But this time he made the rounds more quickly, whipping up the tension that permitted him to raise his prices; he paid no more compliments

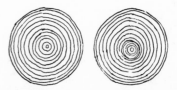

and left no time for any exchanges of knives; a calculated haste entered into his movements. "On your mark, get set," he shouted. At "Go" he tore the napkin off the basket, reached into the basket, and handed out, dispensed, distributed among the multitude... onions—onions such as were represented, golden-yellow and slightly stylized, on his shawl, plain ordinary onions, not tulip bulbs, but onions such as women buy in the market, such as the vegetable woman sells, such as the peasant, the peasant's wife, or the hired girl plants and harvests, onions such as may be seen, more or less faithfully portrayed in the still lifes of the lesser Dutch masters. Such onions, then, Schmuh dispenses among his guests until each had an onion and no sound could be heard but the purring of the stoves and the whistling of the carbide lamps. For the grand distribution of onions was followed by silence. Into which Ferdinand Schmuh cried, "Ladies and gentlemen, help yourselves." And he tossed one end of his shawl over his left shoulder like a skier just before the start. This was the signal.

The guests peeled the onions. Onions are said to have seven skins. The ladies and gentlemen peeled the onions with the paring knives. They removed the first, third, blond, golden-yellow, rust-brown, or better still, onion-coloured skin, they peeled until the onion became glassy, green, whitish, damp, and

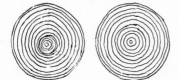

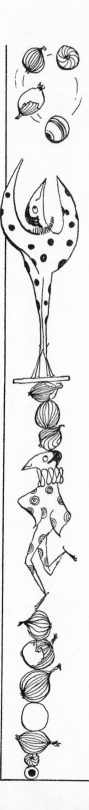

water-sticky, until it smelled, smelled like an onion. Then they cut it as one cuts onions, deftly or clumsily, on the little chopping boards shaped like pigs or fish; they cut in one direction and another until the juice spurted or turned to vapour—the older gentlemen were not very handy with paring knives and had to be careful not to cut their fingers; some cut themselves even so, but didn't notice it—the ladies were more skillful, not all of them, but those at least who were housewives at house, who knew how one cuts up onions for hash-brown potatoes, or for liver with apples and onion rings; but in Schmuh's onion cellar there was neither, there was nothing whatever to eat, and anyone who wanted to eat had to go elsewhere, to the "Fischl," for instance, for at the Onion Cellar onions were only cut. Why all these onions? For one thing, because of the name. The Onion Cellar had its specialty: onions. And moreover, the onion, the cut onion, when you look at it closely. . . but enough of that, Schmuh's guests had stopped looking, they could see nothing more, because their eyes were running over and not because their hearts were so full; for it is not true that when the heart is full the eyes necessarily overflow, some people can never manage it, especially in our century, which in spite of all the suffering and sorrow will surely be known to posterity as the tearless century. It was this

drought, this tearlessness that brought those who could afford it to Schmuh's Onion Cellar, where the host handed them a little chopping board—pig or fish—a paring knife for eighty pfennigs, and for twelve marks an ordinary field-, garden-, and kitchen-variety onion, and induced them to cut their onions smaller and smaller until the juice—what did the onion juice do? It did what the world and the sorrows of the world could not do: it brought forth a round, human tear. It made them cry. At last they were able to cry again. To cry properly, without restraint, to cry like mad. The tears flowed and washed everything away. The rain came. The dew. Oskar has a vision of floodgates opening. Of dams bursting in the spring floods. What is the name of that river that overflows every spring and the government does nothing to stop it?

From *Harriet the Spy* by Louise Fitzhugh. [1]

Harriet felt so grumpy she knocked off work for the day. That night after supper she tried to practice being an onion. She started by falling down several times, making a great bumping noise each time. The idea was to fall in a rolling way the way an onion would and

1   Excerpt from *Harriet the Spy* by Louise Fitzhugh. Copyright © 1964 by Louise Fitzhugh. By permission of Harper & Row, Publishers, Inc.

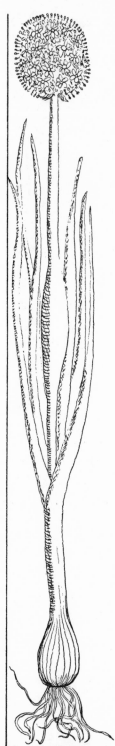

then roll around in a complete circle several times, then roll slowly to a stop the way an onion would if you put it down on a table. Harriet rolled around and bumped into a chair, knocking it over.

Her mother came to the door. She looked down at Harriet lying there with the chair on top of her. "What are you doing?" she asked mildly.

"Being an onion."

Her mother picked the chair up off Harriet's chest. Harriet didn't move. She was tired.

"What in the world is all that noise I hear in here?"

"I told you. I'm being an onion."

"It's a pretty noisy onion."

"I can't help it. I can't do it right yet. Miss Berry says when I do it right, I won't make a sound."

"Oh, it's for the Christmas pageant. . . is that it?"

"Well, you don't think I'd just be an onion all on my own, do you?"

"None of your lip there, girl. Get up and let me see what you have to do."

Harriet got up and fell over, then rolled and rolled around until suddenly she rolled right under the bed. She came out full of dust mice.

Mrs. Welsch looked horrified. "That terrible maid. I'm going to fire her tomorrow."

She looked at Harriet, who stood ready to fall again. "That's the clumsiest dance I ever saw. Miss Berry assigned this?"

"Miss Berry assigned the onion part. I'm making up the DANCE," Harriet said pointedly.

"Oh," said Mrs. Welsch discreetly.

Harriet fell over again, this time rolling away almost into the bathroom.

Mr. Welsch came into the room. "What's going on in here? It sounds like someone hitting a punching bag."

"She's being an onion."

They stood watching Harriet fall over and over again.

Mr. Welsch put his pipe in his mouth and crossed his arms. "According to Stanislavsky you have to feel like an onion. Do you feel like an onion?"

"Not in the least," said Harriet.

"Oh, come on. What are they teaching you in school these days?" Mrs. Welsch started to laugh.

"No, I'm serious. There's a whole school downtown that's probably rolling all over the floor right this minute."

"I never WANTED to be an onion," Harriet said from the floor.

"And it's a good thing. How many parts do you think are written for onions these days?" Mr. Welsch laughed. "I don't imagine you did want to be an onion. For that matter, who knows if an onion does either."

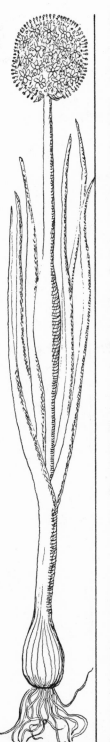

Mrs. Welsch laughed up at him. "You're so smart. Let's see *you* fall like an onion."

"Don't mind if I do," said Mr. Welsch, and putting down his pipe, he fell solidly to the floor. The floor shook.

"Honey! Did you hurt yourself?"

Mr. Welsch just lay there flat. "No," he said quietly, "but it's not as easy as it looks." He lay there breathing. Harriet took another fall just to keep him company.

"Why don't you get up, honey?" Mrs. Welsch stood over him with a worried look on her face.

"I'm trying to feel like an onion. The closest I can get is a scallion."

Harriet tried to feel like an onion. She found herself screwing her eyes up tight, wrapping her arms around her body, then buckling her knees and rolling to the ground.

"My God, Harriet, are you sick?" Mrs. Welsch rushed over to her.

Harriet rolled round and round the room. It wasn't bad at all, this being an onion. She bumped into her father, who started to laugh. She couldn't keep her face screwed up and laughed at him.

Her father started being an onion in earnest, rolling and rolling. Harriet suddenly jumped up and started to write in her notebook:

I WONDER WHAT IT WOULD BE LIKE TO BE A TABLE OR A CHAIR OR A

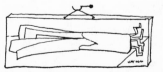

BATHTUB OR ANOTHER PERSON. I
WONDER WHAT OLE GOLLY WOULD SAY
TO THAT. OLE GOLLY LOOKED LIKE A
BIRD WITH TEETH, BUT I THINK I
REALLY LOOK A LITTLE LIKE AN ONION.
I WISH SHE WOULD COME BACK.

MORE ALLIUM FESTIVALS

1. Blessing of the Seeds—a ceremony
    held in Orange County, N.Y., at
    onion planting time.
2. St. Gregory's Day, March 12—known
    as Gregory Great Onion. The day is
    onion planting time in Great Britain.
3. Garlic and Basil Festival—a harvest
    festival held on July 26, St. Anne's
    Day at Tours, France.
4. The Onion Fair at Le Mans, France—
    another harvest festival held in August
    or September each year.
5. The Gilroy Garlic Festival—a new
    harvest festival held in August that
    promises to rival the great European
    garlic festivals. Take a plane to
    California, if you're not already living
    there, and see for yourself.
6. The Polish Dozynki—In August in

Orange County, N.Y., all those seeds planted at the Blessing of the Seeds have grown into onions ready for harvesting. This festival, held on the Feast of the Assumption ("Our Lady of the Flowers"), celebrates onions! The Queen of the festival has herself worked in the onion fields. The pageant figures—Lord and Lady of the Manor—are presented with baskets and wreaths of onions. And the *Trojak Cebulowy* or Onion Dance is performed. Here is Betty Jane Wright's description of it:

Little girls in white with kelly green skirts and matching bonnets, and little boys in blue overalls and straw hats depicted the activities of the onion grower. To a jaunty rhythm, they interpreted the sowing of the seeds, weeding and cultivating, picking and preparing onions for market, selling and returning from market with full pockets.

So, look once again at that onion in your hand and think a little bit about the universe.

And then you'll be ready for a touch of science.

2.

ALLIUM CHEMISTRY

What a garlick Breath my Lady Springwell had!
John Dryden, *The Wild Gallant* (1663)

As far as we're all concerned, there are two important questions about alliums:

1. Why do they stink (and why do they make *you* stink)?
2. Why do they make you cry?

Actually, many of us don't think alliums stink at all, but rather that they are pungent, aromatic, flavorful, what have you. However, we all do agree that they have a strong smell, and one that seems to hang around for rather a bit after we've eaten them. At any rate, the smell results in that lovely flavor. And it's the chemistry that results in the smell.

To put it simply, the alliums all have their

characteristic odor because of a variety of *sulfur compounds* present in all of them. Mostly everyone has smelled or heard of the odor of rotten eggs that sulfur produces when burned and combined with certain elements. Well, when sulfur combines with certain other elements, it smells like onions. The interesting thing is that onions, garlic and company do not contain the same sulfur compounds, a fact that has been only recently discovered. For example, it was thought that the volatile oil (an oil which quickly becomes a gas at a low temperature) which causes the odor and taste of onions and garlic was *allylpropyl disulfide* (also listed as propyl allyldisulfide), but this oil, while present in garlic, is not the volatile constituent of onions. Furthermore, it is not the major active odor-producing substance in either. Onion oil contains about ten compounds, five of which contain sulfur, the most abundant being *n-propylthiol*. Garlic oil is also made up of sulfur compounds; the main one is *diallyl disulfide*. More on these constituents in a bit. Just remember that in all cases, it is sulfur in some form or another that does the trick.

Now, why do these sulfurous compounds make you smell? Although the mouthwash makers would like you to believe that it's because garlic or onion particles linger in between your teeth and cause the fragrance, they are full of hot air. The fact is the abovementioned oils enter the lungs and are exhaled with every breath. They are also exuded through the pores. The oils are so potent that they can even be absorbed into the body without being eaten. Two examples:

1.   Herbalist Jeanne Rose, wanting to test this fact, put four cloves of garlic in her sock and wore it for a day. She discovered that in seven hours, the garlic could be smelled on her breath.

2.   John Harris cites a letter to *The Lancet*, the British medical journal, mentioning that garlic oil can penetrate the placenta and has been detected on many occasions on the breaths of newborn babies delivered of garlic-eating mothers.

Strong stuff, eh! You can eat a variety of foods after the garlic or onions to cut down the smell—parsley, celery leaves, rue, juniper berries, apples, coffee beans, cardamom and cloves being but a few often mentioned—but these will never entirely eliminate it. Certain cooking techniques will also reduce the odor. And then, of course, you could stick to leeks, shallots and chives, which don't have as strong an aroma. But, the Author's advice is Learn to Love Your Garlicky

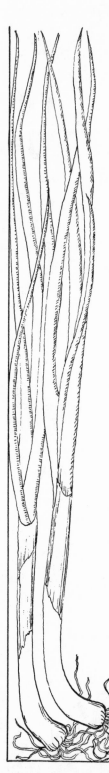

Smell, and Everyone Else Can Go Suck a Leek. This may sound anti-social, but if you can get everyone around you to indulge, nobody will be smellier than anyone else!

Read It and Weep

So now for question two—why do alliums make you cry? The search for the structure and composition of the *lachrymator* (tear-producer) has gone on for some time, with lots of mistakes along the way. In his article, Thomas Maugh states that recently Eric Block of the University of Missouri at St. Louis seems to have come up with the correct information. The answer—another sulfur compound, folks: *propanethial S-oxide!* This volatile compound decomposes so rapidly that Block had to use microwave spectroscopy and other special techniques to isolate it at low temperatures. He found that when the compound is dissolved in water, it hydrolyzes to form *sulfuric acid.* Block's theory is that propanethial S-oxide, freed when onions are peeled or sliced, can dissolve in the small quantities of water always present in the human eye and produce sulfuric acid, which burns and irritates and causes tearing. Refrigerating onions before peeling and peeling them under cold running water reduces tearing because the former reduces the volatility

of the lachrymator, the latter because the water dissolves it.

> *You break the alliin down,*
> *To let the allicin be,*
> *All with that alliinase*
> *To let the allyls go free.*
> *Then there's allithiamine*
> *And selenium too,*
> *Germanium and Gurwitch rays*
> *And boop-boop-be-doo.*
> *Garlic's the stuff that's good for you!*

Allicin, alliin, alliinase! What is all this, you must be thinking. "All this" is the chemical constituents of garlic. No organic substance is a simple combination of ingredients, and garlic is no exception. We are still hazy about what exactly is in garlic and how what's in it works. But there seems to have been more research on it than on the onion. In 1892, P. W. Semmler, a German scientist, attempted to analyze garlic to discover what gives it its odor. He discovered that *diallyl disulfide* makes up sixty percent of the components of garlic oil. Twenty years later, another German scientist, C. Rundquist, was able to extract a crystalline substance from garlic which he thought was a glucoside, and he named it *alliin*. It was some years later that A. Stoll discovered that alliin is not a glucoside, but an *amino acid.* It is also the major active substance in garlic, producing its characteristic garlic odor when mixed with water.

Stoll also extracted *allicin,* which had been discovered in 1944 by C. V. Cavillito. Allicin is a colorless, chemically unstable oil with antibiotic properties. Tadashi Watanabe says that the great germicidal power of allicin results from its double ability to oxidize sulfur. Allicin is the result when alliin reacts with an enzyme known as *alliinase,* also discovered by Stoll. Then allicin, in turn, breaks down to form *diallyl disulfide* (the source of that smell) and *allyl thiosulfinate,* which appears to be the antibiotic essence of garlic. The antibiotic property is extremely important and apparently effective, as the next chapter will show.

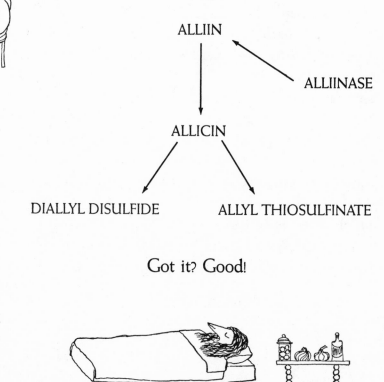

ALLIIN

ALLIINASE

ALLICIN

DIALLYL DISULFIDE   ALLYL THIOSULFINATE

Got it? Good!

Now, garlic has a lot of other good things in it as well. For example, when the allicin in garlic reacts with Vitamin B1, it produces *allithiamine*, a substance which seems to preserve the vitamin for animal use and increase the efficacy of Vitamin B1, thus preventing and curing diseases such as beriberi. Allicin can also combine with proteins and change their structure to make them easier to digest. So, garlic is a good accompaniment to meat, fish, eggs, beans and other protein foods. Garlic also contains two elements which are toxic in large amounts, but appear to be beneficial in small quantities—*selenium*, a substance which is related to Vitamin E and which is thought to prevent clotting, to normalize blood pressure, to prevent infections and to slow aging, and *germanium*, thought to be a cancer preventative. Studies indicate that garlic also contains anti-coagulants, anti-hemolytics (against anemia) and anti-arthritic and sugar-regulating factors making it useful in connection with diabetes, blood clots and a variety of other diseases and disorders. And, like onions, marjoram and green chilies, garlic also possesses an antioxidant property. This means it preserves food. It is therefore used in food preparation in many countries to prevent spoilage.

Furthermore, as if all this were not enough, garlic also contains some Vitamins C and A (but

not a lot in the bulb—only the leaves have much) and a considerable amount of minerals (manganese, copper, iron, zinc, sulfur, calcium, aluminum, chlorine, and the abovementioned germanium and selenium). Watanabe claims that a viscous substance in garlic, which is a kind of glucose, is nutritious and probably helpful in other ways. And garlic also gives off Gurwitsch rays.

A Garlic   *An M-ray*   *A Gurwitsch*

Not too long ago, Dr. S.S. Nehru, president of the Agriculture-in-India Science Congress, conducted experiments in an attempt to discover why onion poultices help inflammations of the throat and sinuses. In his research, he found that onions emit an electrical energy which can pass through cellophane or quartz, but not glass, lead, iron or aluminum. This radiation seems to be the M-rays that Professor Gurwitsch, a Russian electro-biologist, discovered in 1920. Gurwitsch claimed that these ultra-violet rays, emitted by onions, garlic and ginseng, have the ability to stimulate cell growth during cell division or *mitosis*. So he called these *mitogenetic* or M-rays. Moreover, the radiation produced by these plants is similar to the one produced by penicillin. This all means that electrical energy in onions and garlic may be responsible for at least some of its healing and rejuvenating powers. Scientists following Gurwitsch's research have found similar results, but his work has been rejected in Britain and America. Perhaps with increased interest in herbal medicine, these countries will look again at Gurwitsch and his rays.

This increased interest has indeed led to a fascinating brand new discovery in the chemical structure of onions (and, probably, the other alliums). Moses Attrep, Jr., of East Texas State University has claimed to have isolated *prostaglandin* A_1. Prostaglandins are a little understood group of hormones which seem to do almost everything from causing headaches to curing them to inducing abortion. Prostaglandin A_1 is known to help high blood pressure. Intrigued by reports that onions could reduce hypertension, Attrep used chromatography and mass spectroscopy to study them and discovered the prostaglandin, the first time it—or any prostaglan-

din—has been shown to be present in a plant! Chances are garlic will be found to contain even more of it than onions as it is a more potent anti-hypertensive, as well as a stronger antibiotic and antiseptic.

This is not to knock onions or leeks, chives, shallots, et al. Virtually all of the alliums contain some allicin and therefore they have some germicidal effects. And all of the alliums have a certain amount of vitamins and a good amount of minerals. All are useful sources of carbohydrates, calcium, phosphorus, sodium, potassium, manganese, iron and, of course, sulfur, as well as Vitamins of the B complex, and Vitamins C and A, to some extent, and traces of iodine, zinc and other minerals. All are fairly low in calories. And they all taste good.

So, it's easy to see that there's got to be something good about these alliums. Something healthy.

. . . and that's just what the next chapter is about.

3.

MEDICINAL USES

An allium a day keeps the doctor away.

A Writer

or

Dr. Singer's Guaranteed, One in a Million Miracle Cure

Eat leeks in Lide [March] and ramsies in May,
And all the year after physicians may play.

Cuban Technique for Avoiding Jaundice
Take 13 cloves of garlic and string them on a cord. Wear it around your neck for 13 days. At midnight on the 13th day, go to a crossroads. Take off the necklace and fling it behind you. Run home as fast as you can without looking back. You will be safe from jaundice.

To Awaken a Patient from 'Herbal Anesthesia'
Mix onion and vinegar and pour it into the

112

patient's mouth. He will wake presently. (A 14th Century Welsh recipe)

Going Bald?
Rub raw onions into your scalp every night and watch your hair thicken and grow.

This may all sound like a bunch of old wives' tales, but why put down old wives. That bulb you picked up at the beginning of this book is more than a plant with an interesting history. It appears to be a genuine medicinal wonder. Onions and garlic, in particular, have been used throughout history with considerable success to treat a variety of ailments ranging from toothache to cancer. It's not surprising that alliums have been thought to be magical.

Five thousand years ago, the Egyptians and the Jews knew that onions and other alliums had powerful medicinal properties. They ate and drank various onion, garlic and leek concoctions and wore them around their necks to prevent disease; they recorded these cures and preventatives in scrolls and paintings. In Asis, an ancient clay tablet was found with the following inscription: "Let a cow starve for three days, then give it one part garlic and two parts grass; its milk can then be used as an anthelmintic [dewormer]." The Codex Ebers, a medical papyrus discovered by German Egyptologist George Ebers and pub-

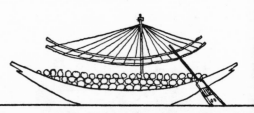

lished in 1878, contains eight hundred therapeutic formulas, twenty-two of which mention garlic. One of garlic's most common uses was for the treatment of insect and arachnid (spider and scorpion) bites, a practice that exists today in many countries, as in this:

Traditional Welsh Cure for Spider Bites

Take nine cloves of garlic and peel carefully, a spoonful of treacle, a quart of a new strong ale, mix these together and give them to the patient to drink freely. At the same time cover him with an abundance of clothes so that he may perspire well. If he can retain this position for an hour he will escape even though the integument had become mottled. This medicament is also useful for a person bitten by an adder.

And *The Talmud*, the Jewish book of law, also recommends garlic and other alliums for numerous problems—from menstrual difficulties to inflammations.

The Sumerians, Babylonians and Assyrians apparently used alliums similarly. One common practice which persists today in these and other desert countries is the rubbing of garlic on people's noses to cool and protect themselves from *simooms* and *siroccos* (hot winds). And in these

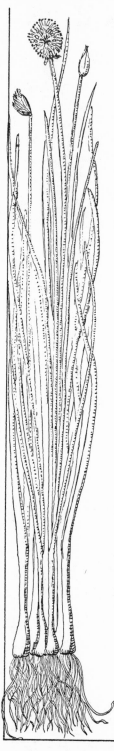

and other countries, garlic and onions have been used as contraceptives. The ancient Chinese, too, found garlic, leeks, onions and chives particularly helpful in intestinal, urinary and respiratory problems. A unique Chinese use of garlic was—and is—*moxibustion* or *moxa*, a technique related to acupuncture in which burning cones of mugwort are applied to the body at various points. In the treatment of various respiratory, rheumatic and neuralgic troubles, moxa specialists often place a small slice of garlic between the cone and the skin. The result is supposed to be something like using *Ben-Gay* or any other counter-irritant—warming and soothing. The basis for this and other forms of Oriental medicine is that in the early stages, diseases are caused by blockage or imbalances of the body's energy flow or *Chi*. This flow can be stimulated by acupuncture, moxibustion and various herbs such as garlic. It's sort of like saying the good energy from garlic and other alliums fights bad energies. Gurwitsch and his rays certainly suggest this possibility. And given the track record of both acupuncture and garlic, who are we Westerners to sneer at such an idea?

Perhaps the largest body of *materia medica* concerning the alliums has been handed down to us from the Greeks and Romans. Most of our English herbals are based directly on information in these classical texts. The Greek physicians Hippocrates and Dioscorides left extensive records of their use of alliums to treat coughs, bites, worms, menstrual problems, skin diseases, wounds, toothaches and even epilepsy. Celsus found them useful for reducing fever. Aristotle thought garlic was good for constipation and hydrophobia (rabies), but bad for the eyes—perhaps because it makes them tear. As was mentioned in Part 1, Pliny, the Roman naturalist, was a great allium advocate, who suggested this remedy for garlic breath: "If a man would not have his breath stink with eating of garlic, let him do no more but take a beetroot roasted in the embers, and eat it after, it shall extinguish that hot and strong flavour." Aëtius declared that garlic could forestall an attack of gout, especially in October. And Galen, perhaps the greatest Roman physician of all, called garlic a "medicine of the poor" and advocated onions for phlegmatic (apathetic, passive) people, but not for active, lively ones. His ideas suggested the concept of the *Four Humours*—popular in Europe for centuries.

THE FOUR HUMOURS

A personality quiz:
Your best friend tells you he/she is going out with your girl friend/boy friend. Do you:

a) Get depressed and gaze longingly into the river.
b) Go find another boy friend/girl friend.
c) Shrug.
d) Slug him/her.

Answers:

If you chose *a*, you are a *melancholy* type, full of *yellow bile*. If you chose *b*, you have a *sanguine* personality and you are full of *blood*. If *c* was your selection, you are definitely *phlegmatic* and full of *phlegm*. Finally, if you picked *d*, you are a *choleric* (angry) person and you're loaded with *black bile*.

These humours also correspond to the four elements—fire, air, water and earth—like so:

Black bile (Choleric)—*hot, dry—fire*
Blood (Sanguine)—*hot, moist—air*
Phlegm (Phlegmatic)—*cold, moist—water*
Yellow bile (Melancholy)—*cold, dry—earth*

According to believers in the Four Humours, choleric folks shouldn't eat alliums because they are hot foods, while phlegmatic folks should. The Author is not certain what sanguine or melancholy types are supposed to devour, but guesses the latter should eat alliums, while the former should not. At any rate, this theory explains why certain Medieval man-uscripts suggest leeks for cold temperaments, old

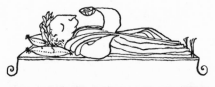

people and those living in the North, as well as
almost everyone during the winter, and why they
say things such as, "To neutralize the hot danger
of leeks on the brain and senses, take with sesame
oil and with oil of sweet almonds," and "Onions
are also dangerous and can cause headaches.
Neutralize with vinegar and milk."

Another theory popular during the Middle
Ages and influenced by the Greeks and Romans
was the *Doctrine of Signatures*, which stated that the
shapes and colors of plants indicated what they
were good or bad for. This doctrine comes from
the lovely idea that everything is connected in a
meaningful relationship, and that God stamps
signatures on plants so that people may know
how to use them. Thus, in Lauremberg's *Apparatus
Plantarium*:

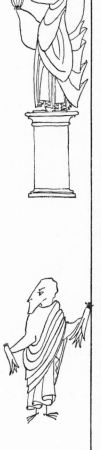

> The seed of Garlic is black; it obscures the
> eyes with blackness and darkness. This is to be
> understood of healthy eyes. Those which are
> dull through vicious humidity from these Garlic
> drives this viciousness away. The tunic of garlic
> is ruddy; it expels blood... It has a hollow
> stalk, and it helps affections of the windpipe.

Likewise, because the onion is round, it has been
associated with the *head* and the relief of its ills.

Helvetius, the 18th century French philoso-
pher, had a different theory. He identified plants

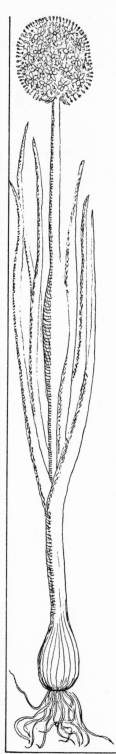

with parts of the body—chives with the stomach; garlic with the hands, fingers and nerves. He also identified garlic with war because of its spearlike shape.

Obviously, these theories, though charming, are not terribly accurate and should not be compared to genuine medicine such as acupuncture or the many fine uses of herbs that have come down to us through the ages.

In the Middle Ages, the successful use of the alliums continued. The Spanish rabbi and physician Maimonides recommended garlic for scorpion bites. "The Reverend Maister" Aleris (and lots of others, as shown in Part 1) used garlic and other alliums to keep away the plague. Alexander Neckam, a 12th century writer, suggested garlic as a palliative for the heat of the sun in field labor. And the following Medieval complexion aids may or may not have worked:

> An Onion, dipped in honey and salt and mixed with hen grease, will remove red and blue spots from the skin.

> Onion juice added to honey and white wax will rid you of wrinkles.

In the golden age of herbals, the opinion about alliums became sharply divided. There were the supporters—Queen Elizabeth I's surgeon, William Clowes, used onion juice to cure

gun powder burns. And before him, Ambroise Paré (1517-1590) used it for gunshot wounds. Cole, in his *Art of Simpling*, says that garlic makes cocks and horses strong. Hyll wrote of garlic, "But yet in wynter it is verye food for fleumatike persons to eate thereof, if it be good propertieth also it hath, for as much as it greatly healpeth agaynst all poysons if it be eaten, or otherwise, fyne brused and mingled with wine and so to be drunke." But he, like others, did not recommend it for the choleric. And there were the detractors. Culpeper, perhaps the best known herbalist of his day and after, wrote:

> Many authors quote many diseases this [garlic] is good for, but conceal its vices. Its heat is very vehement, and all vehement hot things send up but ill-flavoured vapours to the brain. In choleric men it will add fuel to the fire; in men oppressed by melancholy, it will attenuate the humour, and send up strong fancies, and as many strange visions to the head; therefore let it be taken inwardly with great moderation; outwardly you may make more bold with it.

Small wonder that garlic fell into disfavor in Great Britain! Culpeper didn't even advise it for the melancholy!

To put us in a Better Humour about garlic and company, let's look at:

Allium Astrology

Mars

Planet of war, energy, detection, etc. Rules garlic, leeks, onions, etc. Therefore, these plants are good for ARIES people who are ruled by Mars.

However, when giving herbs as medicine, according to medical astrology, it is necessary to look at each individual's chart and to use the herbs respective of the aspects in each chart. For example, if Mars is afflicting Mercury, give Mars herbs like onions and garlic. But if Mars is afflicting Jupiter, creating impure blood, liver diseases, a liability to burns and accidents or whatever, give Venusian herbs rather than Martial ones. Similarly, if Uranus is afflicted with Saturn, causing cold, rheumatic and nervous disorders, or if Saturn and the Moon are afflicted, give alliums. Garlic and other alliums are also important to Capricorn and Aquarius to balance the lethargy of these signs. And if you can't make sense of all this, just ask your local astrologer to explain it to you.

Although the British may have turned medical thumbs down to alliums, the rest of Europe didn't. The Turks ate onions to prevent goiter (an abnormality of the thyroid gland caused by lack of iodine). French doctors in Molière's time prescribed onions for kidney stones and dropsy (a fluid retention disease). Carmine, an acquaintance of the Author's, says that when he was growing up on a farm in Italy, roasted garlic was rubbed on his feet to reduce the callouses and soreness—a practice that is probably quite old. The long-lived Abkhasians ate, and still eat, large quantities of garlic. In a recent study about them, it was shown that forty percent of the men and thirty percent of the women over the age of ninety could see well enough to thread a needle without glasses. In Serbia, every autumn, old and lame folk go on a pilgrimage to the forest to eat the *ceremissa*, a wild garlic, and return home invigorated. To this day in Poland and Russia, where garlic and other alliums have a special place in medicine, pious Jews break their fasts on bread and raw garlic. The incidence of cancer among them is extremely low. And Russian *znakhari* (folk medicine healers) use garlic for arteriosclerosis (hardening of the arteries), high blood pressure, coughs and colds, nervous spasms and seizures, earaches, toothaches, stomach aches, headaches, gout, rheumatism, fevers, convulsions, fainting, epilepsy, internal and external parasites, ringworm, acne, hemorrhoids, tuberculosis, and as a tonic. No wonder garlic is called the *Russian penicillin.*

In Asia and Africa too, the alliums were and are important to medicine. The Berbers of North Africa bake garlic in bread as a cold cure. The Malayans use garlic juice for septicemia (blood poisoning) and, mixed with betel nuts and alum, as eyedrops. In India, garlic is given to hysterical girls to soothe them. And then there's this Eastern cure for toothache (not recommended to people who don't know what they're doing):

Take finely chopped garlic and place it on the underside of the wrist. Bandage firmly and leave for some hours. When a blister forms, remove the bandage. Puncture the blister with a sterilized needle to let the poison drain out. Apply soothing oil to the wrist and bandage. The blistered area will heal in about four days. And the toothache will be unlikely to reoccur for many years.

This cure, which works through the stimulation of the lung meridian of acupuncture, is very similar to an American folk cure:

Split an onion, roast it and bind it while hot on the wrist, over the pulse, on the opposite side from the aching tooth.

A rather more pleasant technique is to put a clove of garlic in your mouth on the infected tooth—a method which is also splendid for colds.

The Americas were also quick to catch on to allium cures. Native Americans long knew of wild onions, garlic and leeks for medicinal purposes. The Cheyenne used wild garlic to treat carbuncles and boils. The Winnebago and Dakota nations found bruised wild onions excellent for wasp and bee stings. The Mohegans, along with many other peoples, made a cold syrup from wild alliums. Hawaiians use *aka'akai* or onions for earaches and to strengthen the eyes. For the latter, onion skin is boiled and cooled and a bit of the fluid drunk as a tea daily. In the Southern U.S., Black herb doctors have used the alliums for a myriad of problems. For example, early twentieth century herbalist Aunt Rhoda prescribed a mixture of English plantain and garlic for coughs and kidney trouble. And in Mexico, *curanderos* or herb doctors still flourish in many villages and sell a super-garlic—*ajo macho*—as a cure for cancer and onions to guard against venereal disease. Jean Strouse writes that garlic is even used there to end sibling rivalry!

European settlers to America brought along their favorite cures, to be modified by time and history. Cures such as:

FOR EARACHE (C. Kinsley, 1876)
Soak the feet in warm water, roast an onion, and put the heart of it into the ear as warm as can be

borne. Heat a brick and wrap it up, and apply it to the side of the head. When the feet are taken from the water, bind roasted onions on them. Lard or sweet oil dropped in the ear as warm as can be borne is also good.

FOR VOMITING (C.H. Fowler and W.H. DePuy, 1880)

An old recipe used by a doctor on a very sick patient: Peel a large onion and cut in half. Place one half in each armpit. According to this source: In several attacks since that time have I seen this remedy promptly control the incessant vomiting and relieve the distressing nausea.

FOR COUGHS (Mrs. R.S., 1951)

Take 18 ounces of good onions, and after removing the rind make several incisions but not too deep. Boil together with 14 ounces of moist sugar and 3 ounces of honey in 35 ounces of water, for ¾ hour; strain and bottle. Give 1 tablespoon slightly warmed immediately on attack, and then, according to needs, 5 to 8 tablespoons daily.

FOR HIGH BLOOD PRESSURE (South Carolinian cure)

Put garlic in wine vinegar with lemon juice and Epsom salts. Take one teaspoon every morning for nine days. Or just put garlic in water and take the teaspoon every morning.

FOR POISON IVY (Carrie Funk Koch, *Naturopath*)

Crush several cloves of garlic, place between layers of gauze and apply on sore spots for about thirty minutes.

FOR HAIR LOSS (Dr. John Lust, *The Herb Book*)

Nettle leaves (1 part)
Onion (1 part)
70% alcohol (100 parts)
Soak the leaves and onion in alcohol for several days. Use to massage the scalp daily.

FOR COLDS OR FLU (The Author)

Chop one clove of garlic coarsely. Swallow bit by bit with lots of water. Do this two or three times a day. Drink lots of herbal teas (ginger, sage or comfrey, especially). Keep warm.

It is obvious that as allium folk remedies have parallels throughout the world, word of their efficacy must have spread quickly. Note these similarities:

FOR COUGHS OR CROUP
England

Cover up the patient. Put garlic in his/her socks and let him/her wear them until the fever breaks and the coughing subsides.

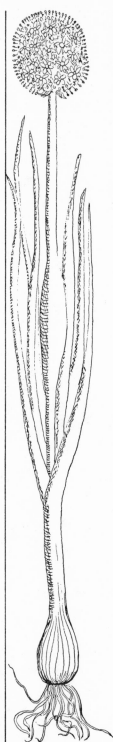

Australia
A cold water compress consisting of a man's handkerchief, well wrung out, is placed around the throat and covered with a warm scarf. As an extra, onions are chopped up and put in a pillow case and the feet of the patient are placed in this and left for as long as necessary.

U.S.
Apply several thicknesses of flannel, wet in hot water, over the throat, as hot as can be borne, and change as often as it cools. Put onion poultices on the feet, after soaking them a little time; lose no time in sending for a physician.

In the U.S., among other countries, we tend to reject what we call "folk remedies" in favor of Modern Medicine. But here are a bunch of doctors (and other folk) who are alliaceous practitioners.[1]

Drs. W.C. Minchin and M. W. Duffie
Garlic is the best individual treatment found to get rid of germs and we believe same to be a specific for the tubercle

1 Note: Since the Author is an ecstatic allium fanatic, all of the research included here says Hooray for Alliums. Some people don't think so highly of these herbs, but the Author doesn't think so highly of these people and prefers not to write about them.

bacillus and for tubercular processes no matter what part of the body is affected.

Dr. M. W. Duffie,
"Tuberculosis Treatment,"
North American Journal of Homeopathy, 1914

At the Metropolitan Hospital in New York, Duffie tested 57 treatments for tuberculosis and found garlic superior to all of them. At the same time in Dublin, Ireland, Dr. Minchin used garlic in a variety of ways to treat tuberculosis, then the worst disease around. He had remarkable success and published his results in *The Lancet*.

Dr. W. I. Marcovici

In 1915, Marcovici had much success using garlic during the war to treat dysentery and other gastrointestinal disorders. He was also one of the first physicians to use garlic pills in treatment. Encouraged by the results, he conducted controlled experiments with rabbits in the 1920's and found that garlic given for three days prior to injections of dysentery toxin protected the animals against a ten-fold dose and that when given at the same time as the toxin, it cured all the rabbits.

Marcovici also worked with elderly patients with high blood pressure and intestinal problems. He claimed that the decrease of hypertension was due not to the ability of garlic to dilate blood vessels, but to purify the intestines.

Numerous other doctors have since studied garlic's effect both on the gastrointestinal and the cardiovascular systems. They confirmed Marcovici's findings that garlic is helpful to the guts. However, all of them agreed that although garlic is good for the innards, it must not be over-indulged in if the stomach or intestines are weak. One must build up garlic consumption. Doctors also agree that garlic lowers high blood pressure, as do onions and other alliums to a lesser degree. However, recent research seems to indicate that garlic does *dilate* blood vessels. And similar studies conducted on onions show the same thing.

Dr. J. Klosa

In the 1940's, Dr. Klosa used garlic oil in a number of experiments to test its effectiveness in respiratory ailments. He found that garlic helped sore throats, congestion, grippe, etc., in hundreds of cases. From these experiments, he postulated that the garlic sulfides combine with viral matter in such a way as to inhibit their activity.

Dr. Ragnar Huss

Huss long believed that "an unimpaired mucous lining of the intestine might give protection from polio." He studied the works of Dr. Meyerhofer, a German biologist, who felt that "intestinal catarrh" is necessary before a person can contract polio, and of Dr. Nöhlen, who used garlic to keep forty-five monkeys in the Düsseldorf Zoo free of intestinal inflammations. Then, in 1937, when it was apparent that a polio epidemic was on the way in Mälmo, Sweden, Huss gave garlic pills to the children in three schools. None of them got polio, while sixty-seven untreated children did.

A Polish Dentist
In 1960, he reported excellent results from the use of garlic oil to treat root canals—that painful dental procedure which often leaves the affected area open to infection. The garlic oil prevented infections in all the patients treated.

The Case of Juanita Lollis
Twenty-one year old Juanita Lollis sneezed almost continuously for six days. A diet of garlic halted the sneezing for several hours. The sneezing, which had been as rapid as fifteen sneezes per minute, resumed. The garlic diet was continued. And then Ms. Lollis finally stopped sneezing.

A Team of Indian Doctors
A casual remark by a patient that in France when a horse develops clots in its legs, it is treated with a diet of garlic and onions, led these doctors to study onions as a possible fibrinolytic (anti-

clotting) agent. They found that the addition of fried or boiled onions to a fat-enriched breakfast not only prevented the decrease of fibrinolysis that normally follows a high fat diet, but actually *increased* it. In another study, Dr. Jain writes that garlic reduces only low-density lipoprotein cholesterol, rather than high-density lipoprotein cholesterol. It is the former that appears to increase heart disease risk.

In a different study, Drs. Jain, Vyas and Mahatma have reported that in experiments with rabbits, garlic juice lowers high blood sugar. It also raises low blood sugar (hypoglycemia). Thus, garlic appears to stabilize the sugar metabolism.

Arteriosclerosis and Heart Disease

Many experiments have been conducted to study the effect of garlic and onions on fatty deposits in the arteries. In one study, it was found that in rabbits in which arteriosclerosis was induced, onions did not lower the level of cholesterol in the blood or prevent the development of arteriosclerosis, while garlic did both.

Recently, German Professor Hans Reuter said that there is proof that garlic helps clear the blood vessels of cholesterol. Tests showed that volunteers fed butter containing fifty grams of garlic oil had a cholesterol level considerably

lower than that of a control group fed butter without garlic. Reuter also said that in Greece, Russia, India and China, where garlic is much eaten, there are significantly fewer cases of arteriosclerosis. But, he added, fresh garlic, and not powder, must be used, since the processed plant loses its healing properties.

A similar study with rats, and then humans, at the University of Minnesota, has led to the same conclusions.

Cancer

Research on the growth-inhibiting action of garlic dates back to 1500 B.C. The Bower Manuscript (450 A.D.) lists garlic as a cure for abdominal tumors.

In 1949, Dr. Hans Von Euler tested pure alliin on rats with tumors. After the injection of alliin, the tumors regressed or even disappeared.

In 1957, Drs. Weisberger and Pensky of Western Reserve University found that when cancerous cells injected into mice were treated with allicin, no deaths occurred among the animals for six months, while untreated mice died in sixteen days. When the mice were injected with virulent cancer and *then* given garlic injections, the development of the malignancy was delayed and, in some cases, prevented.

Many further experiments of this type have

been tried in Japan, India, China and Russia, and they all yield promising results. Dr. K. Asai of Japan feels that it is the *germanium* in garlic that cures or prevents cancer. He cites the low incidence of cancer among garlic-eating peoples.

Dr. K. Halwax

In a recent research study, Halwax showed that garlic extract can be used to treat chronic anemia. Other studies have also shown onions to be effective. However, there is some evidence that anemic patients can become more anemic if they eat excessive amounts of raw garlic or onions. Dr. Gruhgit fed dogs daily on a large amount of onions and found that at the end of seven days there was destruction of red blood corpuscles. However, he also found that if the diet were continued, tolerance was established with no further increase of anemia.

Drs. Ikezoe and Kitahara

One of the most virulent types of poisons that has threatened us in recent years is heavy-metal poisoning from pollution, fish contamination, industrial work, etc. Kitahara and Ikezoe conducted controlled studies on rabbits and humans. They observed heavy metal poisoning resulting in the destruction of erythrocyte (a certain red blood cell) membrane. Then they dosed a group exposed to the poisons with garlic extract. They

found that the garlic protected the membrane. Other studies in Russia and Japan have suggested the same detoxification properties.

Yoshio Kato's Garlic Spraying Machine— The Ultimate in Old Herbs and New Technology

For many years, Yoshio Kato has used garlic to treat a multitude of diseases. He claims success with stomach and other cancers, gastritis, gastric ulcer, weak stomachs, heart problems, hypertension, tuberculosis, pneumonia, tonsillitis, asthma, numerous skin afflictions, neuralgia, menstrual problems, parasites, and other disorders. Originally, Kato used five primary curative methods, depending on the disease:

1. Grated garlic in an oblate, taken orally.
2. Garlic preserved in miso (soy bean paste), taken orally.
3. Application of grated garlic to the affected part.
4. Application of slices of garlic.
5. Garlic juice for gargling.

Now, to these methods, he has added the "Flow-Leben" (Life-Flow) system, which took him twenty years to develop. Flow-Leben is a machine which sprays a 70-100% garlic solution depending on the particular ailment. Each patient first

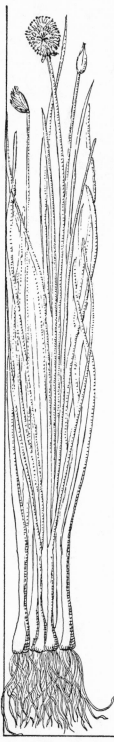

134

takes a dry hot bath to open the pores, then steps into the machine for a garlic shower. This is followed by a cold shower to close the pores and let the garlic work. Kato says he has had even better success with Flow-Leben plus the oral ingestion of garlic than with just the latter alone. In addition to curing the abovementioned diseases, Kato says the garlic spraying machine can also help "whiplash" for which there has previously been no really good treatment. So far, Flow-Leben exists only in Japan, but patents have been granted in other countries and Kato has a vision of setting up a treatment center in every major city in the world.

If all this sounds like science fiction, just remember that laser beams and body scanners sounded impossible just a few years ago. And it was just in this century that *digitalis*, extracted from foxgloves and long used by herbalists, was recognized as a major treatment in heart disease. So, the combination of old herbs and new technology may be the wave of the future, which shouldn't surprise us.

Other Doctors on Garlic

Dr. Paavo Airola may well be this country's foremost medical garlic evangelist. A nutritionist and naturopathic physician, Airola has personally used garlic with much success to treat patients with diarrhea and other intestinal problems such as dysentery and dyspepsia, asthma, high blood pressure, sore throats and colds, and worms (garlic has long been used to expel round and thread worms from the intestines). He recommends eating from one to three small cloves of raw garlic in conjunction with other food or garlic pills with meals everyday.

Dr. Tadashi Watanabe feels that garlic is useful in forms besides raw. Raw garlic is the most potent, he says, but some people have trouble digesting it. For them, he suggests pickled garlic (in vinegar or soy sauce), which preserves most of its effectiveness, but cuts down on its harshness. For people in very poor health, Watanabe feels fried or broiled garlic is good. Cooking destroys the alliinase, but not the alliin in the garlic. Finally, Watanabe says raw garlic in vegetable juice is a good way to get all the benefits without burning your mouth.

WHY DO ALLIUMS MAKE ME FIT AS A FIDDLE?

Who Knows? Well, who knows for sure? No one. There are, once again, many theories. The prostaglandin discovery discussed in the previous chapter, as well as the vitamins, the elements of

selenium and germanium and the sulfur compounds present in alliums may all have something to do with alliaceous antibiosis. Or it may be the Gurwitsch rays. Or perhaps it is what Professor Virtanen, the Finnish Nobel prize winner in medicine, suggests—natural aerosols given off by allium bulbs which kill bacteria. We do know from recent studies such as Dr. Klosa's that the sulfides in allium oil seem to inhibit enzymes in micro-organisms, which both prevents them from synthesizing protein and stops their respiration. Bacteria, viruses and other pests have been shown to become immobile very quickly after being hit with a dose of garlic or onion oil. Unfortunately, more than this we are not clear about. Perhaps further studies will give us the answers.

In the recent past, such studies were frowned upon because herbal medicine was seen as old-fashioned. But as Professor George Sarton says, "It is easy to make fun of medieval recipes; it is more difficult and may be wiser to investigate them." And now, a number of doctors and other medical practitioners agree with him. They point out that while modern antibiotics can destroy helpful bacteria and other microorganisms along with the harmful ones, garlic, onions, leeks and all may let the good flourish while wiping out only the bad. Therefore, folks who complain that

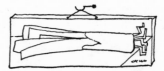

garlic, for example, is not as potent as penicillin should also realize that; A) Garlic is not dangerous, while penicillin and other wonder drugs can be; B) Garlic is part of a holistic system of health which in our Cure-It-And-Run culture is not widely practiced or understood. A) means that the alliums are wholesome foods that do not have a record of harming the body. As Airola writes:

> I have studied the diets of Russians and Bulgarians, where onions and garlic are consumed in astronomical quantities. Not a single case of garlic poisoning has ever been known among them.[1]

B) has even larger implications. That is that garlic, onions, leeks, chives, etc., are not panaceas—cure-alls. They are to be eaten as part of a total program of good nutrition. In other words, you can't expect to exist on McDonald's hamburgers and Coca-Cola and figure that garlic will cure all the ills such rotten eating habits incur. As Hippocrates wrote:

---

1 There are people elsewhere who complain that alliums upset their stomachs. There is also a recorded case in the U.S. of a person who found that garlic decreased the efficiency of the Vitamin E pills he was taking. But alliums have not poisoned anyone. Overindulgence should always be avoided—but what is overindulgence for one person is not so for another. Therefore, it is best to know your own tolerances for any food before you stuff yourself with it.

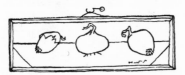

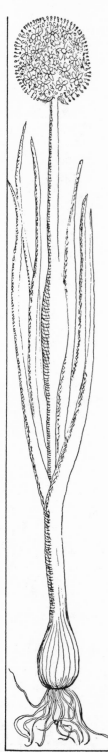

Let your food be your medicine—
Let your medicine be your food.
Moreover, herbal and nutritional medicine do not work overnight, the way Tetracycline or Ampicillin might. Their changes are slower—but more lasting and positive. Translated, this means that a clove of garlic is not equal to a capsule of penicillin, but a clove of garlic *every day* may help your body function better and be healthier in the long run than penicillin ever would. In answer to writers like Berton Roueché who claim that garlic and other alliums work only by the Placebo Effect (which is, if you think they are going to work, then they do)—if a placebo can be so effective as to wipe out colds, cancer and callouses, then UP WITH PLACEBOS!

The Author *is not* suggesting that Western medicine is invalid or that we should never take antibiotics or that doctors don't know what they're doing. Nor is she saying that you should run out and eat alliums and all your troubles will vanish. What she *is* saying is that herbal medicine represents the combined empirical knowledge of many cultures over many centuries in their ongoing struggle against disease and should not be lightly dismissed. She is also saying that an allium a day pretty much never hurts anybody—and may very well help.

Now, perhaps you will be able to look at the following compendium of alliaceous remedies with new eyes and a more open mind.

MORE CURES THAT SMELL

19th Century Cure for Gout
A clove of garlic eaten night and morning.

For Asthma
Chop garlic and put on thin bread and butter. Eat just before going to bed.

For Chest Congestion
Chop garlic cloves and mix with vaseline. Let the vaseline melt. Stir the mixture and cool. Massage into the chest and back several times a day.

For Stuffed Nose and Head
Keep half an onion by your bedside. Sniff deeply when you feel clogged. Eat hot, spicy foods with garlic and chilies to help break up the congestion.

For Nosebleeds
Using a garlic press, squeeze the juice from 2 or 3 cloves of garlic on to some gauze or clean cloth which has been soaked in vinegar. Roll the gauze into a plug and put it into your nostril. Your eyes will tear, but the bleeding will stop.

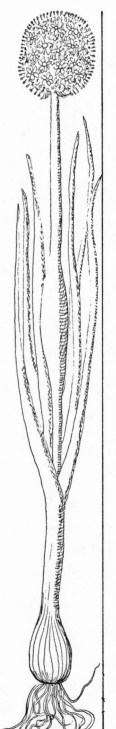

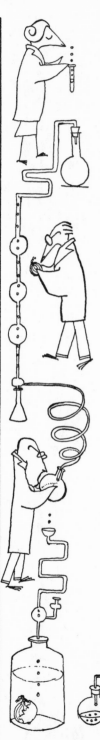

For Bronchitis
Steam whole cloves of garlic, or press the juice into steaming water. Then inhale the vapors deeply.

A Cough Syrup
Peel and slice garlic cloves and put in a bowl. Cover with honey. In a while, a syrup will have formed. Take one teaspoon several times a day.

Another Cough Syrup (Welsh/English)
Boil onions in molasses. Take one teaspoon several times a day.

For Pneumonia (Traditional Welsh)
Take wool from a black sheep. Cover with fried onions, or sometimes mustard and egg white instead. Apply to the chest.

For Breaking Carbuncles and Boils
Chop onions. Mix with black treacle. Make into a poultice. Place on the carbuncle or boil and leave for as long as necessary.

For Earache
Put a peeled, uncut clove of garlic in your ear. Let it sit there for several hours.

For Stomach Ache
Mix chives or garlic with yogurt. Eat a bit at a time.

For Acne or Sores

Crush a few cloves of garlic and add to some yogurt. Let stand for several hours. Apply to the pimples or sores.

Mixed with water and strained of the garlic pieces, this liquid, according to herbalist Jeanne Rose, makes a good douche for vaginal problems.

Brain Power and Garlic

Herbalist Sherry Mestel recommends eating raw garlic mixed with raw seeds (sesame, sunflower, pumpkin) and/or raw nuts as a snack or appetizer to boost your memory and mental energy.

A Liver Flush

Mestel also suggests garlic in this treatment for hepatitis:

Juice of 1 lemon   4 cloves of garlic, crushed
1 Tablespoon olive oil

Mix the ingredients and take on an empty stomach. Follow by three cups of tea. (Peppermint is the most soothing.) Wait at least one hour before eating.

For Insomnia (Welsh/English)

Eat two or three raw onions or onion jelly. The latter is made as follows: Shred two or three good-sized onions in a little stock, and stew until tender. Add a squeeze of fresh lemon juice, then

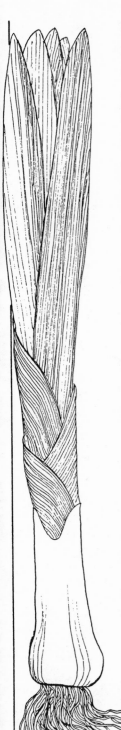

add enough water to make a soup. Boil for ten minutes, then add seasonings, and a small piece of butter.

For Aches and Pains (Traditional Welsh)

"For all kinds of hurtful aches in whatever way they come:

Get parsley, plaintain, daisy, garlic, and grains of Paradise, pound well in a mortar, strain and take the juice in ale. If the patient can obtain beef, he should not eat it when he recovers."

For Kidney Stones (18th Century English)

"The juice of Leeks is a good diuretic and will frequently afford relief in the stone and gravel, when most of the usual remedies fail."

For Cystitis (The Author's Cure)

Chop and swallow four (or more) garlic cloves and two capsules of golden seal each day until the illness is cured. Drink lots of herbal tea—especially comfrey, sage and purifiers such as burdock, alfalfa and dandelion. A comfrey poultice can be used at the opening of the urethra to relieve pain.

For Insect Bites

Crush the leaves of leeks and apply to the bites.

Craig Claiborne's Friend's Cure for Hay Fever

As soon as the hay fever season approaches, eat

twelve cloves of garlic daily in various dishes, at various meals, and you won't sniffle, sneeze or snort.

Joggers' Delight

In a 1978 issue of *Runner's World*, a psychobiologist advises city joggers to eat garlic to offset the bad effects of breathing car exhaust fumes and other pollutants.

ALLIUMS AND VETERINARY MEDICINE

The...onionfish whose body peels into flakes like that bulb, and who zigzags throughout the waves like a leech.
Charles Badham, *Prose Halieutics*, 1854

It is doubtful that the onionfish has therapeutic properties for its predators, but the onion certainly has. Not only have alliums long been used in human medicine but they've been given to pets, domestic animals and zoo denizens for centuries. Seventeeth century writer Gervase Markham (of *The English Hus-wife*) made balls of garlic, aniseed and licorice for horses that had nightmares, just as Gypsies had similar equine remedies. In South Africa, dogs infested with ticks are given chopped garlic in food to make the nasty creatures drop off. In Texas, garlic was fed to wart-plagued steers and it cured them. During a flu epidemic in Cape Town, South Africa, sick baboons were seen burrowing for wild garlic and gorging themselves on it. And let us not forget Dr. Nöhlen and his monkeys, a few pages back.

Garlic especially has been used to treat our canine friends. For bad breath in dogs, kennel owners often give a clove of garlic each day. This may sound absurd, but bad breath is often caused by intestinal problems which garlic is known to clear up. Garlic or onions may also be used to treat mange and other skin diseases, respiratory ailments and worms. In her interesting book, *The Complete Herbal Book for the Dog*, Juliette de Baïracli-Levy suggests giving garlic to nursing bitches daily as a de-wormer. And her following cure for mange seems to be one of the only ones that works:

Take three heads of garlic (about 20 cloves). Slice them. Add two handfuls of finely

cut elder leaves and stalks. Add one quart of cold water; cover; boil. Simmer slowly for half an hour. Remove from heat. Leave for at least seven hours. Rub all over the dog's body. It can also be given internally—2-3 tablespoons every morning and night.

This treatment is coupled with a rigorous program of dieting and bathing (using soap flakes and olive oil soap) once a week which de Baïracli-Levy outlines in her book.

And don't forget, dogs *like* garlic—so slipping a little into Fido's food regularly will not only not hurt him/her, but will probably cause him/her to roll over and grin.

For humans and canines alike—two soups to make you feel healthy:

Garlic Soup

2 tablespoons olive oil	5 cups vegetable or
14 cloves garlic	chicken stock or
Salt and pepper	bouillon
	¼ teaspoon mace

Heat the oil in a pot and fry the garlic for about 8 minutes until it browns. Pour in the stock and add the salt, pepper and mace. Cover the pot and simmer for 15 minutes. Serves 4.

Onion Soup

Touted as a nightcap in New York supper clubs.

3 tablespoons butter

1 tablespoon olive or
vegetable oil

2½ pounds onions,
very thinly sliced

1 teaspoon salt

½ teaspoon sugar

3 tablespoons flour

2 quarts beef stock or
bouillon or robust
vegetable stock

1 cup wine

1 bay leaf

½ teaspoon sage

Salt and pepper to taste

Melt the butter with the oil in a pot. Add the onions. Stir to coat with the butter. Cover the pot and cook over moderate heat for 15-20 minutes, stirring occasionally, until the onions are tender. Uncover the pot. Raise the heat. Stir in the salt and sugar. Cook for 30 minutes, stirring often, until the onions are golden brown. Lower the heat. Stir in the flour and more butter if necessary to make a paste. Cook for about 2 minutes, stirring continuously until the flour is lightly browned. Remove from the heat. Whisk 1 cup of hot stock into the onion mixture. Add the rest of the stock and the wine, bay leaf and sage. Simmer for 30-40 minutes. Season with salt and pepper. Serve with bread and grated Parmesan cheese. Serves 4.

4.

ALLIUM COOKERY

The saucepan without garlic is like a kiss without love.
An Old Spanish Saying

Eating alliums. There's a pleasant thought. There are few vegetable, meat, poultry, fish, egg or cheese dishes that onions, garlic, leeks, chives or shallots will not enhance. They also taste pretty good by themselves. In Part 1 of this book, it has already been noted that cultures the world over eat alliums. In West Africa, while garlic is almost never used, onions (often shallots) are so indispensable in meat or fish dishes that they, along with tomatoes and hot chilies, are called *The Ingredients*. West Africans also use green onions and chives in plenty of dishes. In Europe, Gypsies use little other spicing, but their cooking pots are filled with a good quantity of wild garlic. And throughout many countries and many centuries,

a popular peasant dish has been onions, garlic, wild celery and cheese pounded together. In fact, many of us still think of alliums as essential to fine cooking, possibly because of praise from high-class chefs such as Louis Diat, formerly of New York's Ritz-Carlton:

In times gone by, the sages divided this world into four elements: earth, air, fire and water. If these philosophers had been cooks as well, they would have included a fifth element—garlic. For all good cooks, surely all chefs, would be lost without this pungent vegetable... There is nothing that makes quite the same contribution to an attractive and varied cuisine.

But the truth is that, as we've seen, garlic and other alliums are indigenous to peasant cooking—especially Italian, Spanish, Greek and French provincial cooking—and that it was haute cuisine that made these unfashionable herbs fashionable once again. So fashionable that we couldn't even imagine French cooking without alliums.

When Dumas described the air of Provence as being "particularly perfumed by the refined essence of this mystically attractive bulb," he was talking about garlic. In French country cooking, garlic is present in everything but the dessert.

Where else can you find *Poulet Béarnais*, a chicken dish using forty cloves of garlic, or *Purée de Pommes de Terre a L'ail*, a mashed potato dish calling for two heads of garlic, or the following mayonnaise, *aioli* (*alioli* in Spain):

Aioli

1 slice stale white bread	*4-8 mashed or pressed*
3 tablespoons milk or	*cloves garlic (For*
wine vinegar	*authenticity, mash in*
1 egg yolk	*a mortar)*
¼ teaspoon salt	*1½ cups olive oil*

Remove the crust from the bread. Crumble the bread and soak in the milk or vinegar for 5-10 minutes. Wring out the excess liquid. Place the bread and garlic in a bowl. Pound the two together. Beat in the egg yolk and salt until the mixture is thick and sticky. Blend in the olive oil drop by drop. When the sauce has thickened to heavy cream, you can whisk in the rest of the oil. If you want to thin the aioli, add drops of water or lemon juice. Serve with vegetables, fish dishes, hard-boiled eggs, sandwiches. Makes 2 cups.

If the Aioli Liquifies
Warm a mixing bowl in hot water. Dry. Add 1

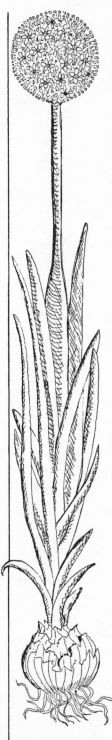

teaspoon of prepared mustard and 1 tablespoon of the aioli. Beat with a whisk for five seconds until it thickens. Add the rest of the aioli gradually and keep beating until it thickens.

Garlic has also been used in not so great cooking. In *La Casa de Luculo O El Arte de Comer* (1937), Spanish gourmet and humorist Julio Camba writes:

Garlic is also commonly used in quantity at country inns to disguise "cat for hare," and in this respect it could be said that garlic is not used to prepare fine food, but to avoid doing so.

What Camba describes was (and is) probably the case in many countries. It is also a practice the Author sneers at.

So here, instead, are some fine examples of allium cookery.[1]

ONION—
The King of Vegetables

Advice on onion cooking:

Let onion atoms lurk within
the bowl,

---

1 Author's Note—The recipes here and elsewhere in this book range from the simple to the not so simple to show the variety of ways alliums can be used in cooking.

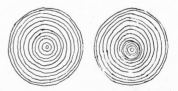

And, scarce-suspected,
animate the whole.

Rev. Sydney Smith

More advice on onion cooking:
Ignore Sydney Smith's advice.
Onions taste great. So why let them be "scarce-suspected"? If you're going to use onions, USE THEM! And that's just what these recipes do.

Braised Onions

1 pound small onions	½ cup stock, bouillon,
1½ tablespoons butter	wine or water
1½ tablespoons oil	Bouquet garni (parsley,
Salt and pepper	bay, thyme, etc.)

Drop the onions in a pot of boiling water for 5-10 seconds so that the skins loosen. Run under cold water. Trim the tops and bottoms so as not to disturb the layers of the onions. Peel. Puncture a cross in each bottom so they'll cook evenly. Brown the onions in a skillet with the butter and oil for 10 minutes. Add the stock, salt and pepper to taste, the bouquet garni and, if you choose, a few lumps of butter. Cover and simmer for 40-50 minutes until the onions are tender and the liquid has largely evaporated. Or bake in a dish at 350° for 40-50 minutes until done. This method is brown-braising. If

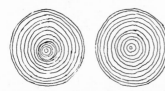

you wish to white-braise the onions, do not brown beforehand. Just put in a white stock, wine or water with the other ingredients and simmer until done. Serves 3-4.

Fried Onion Rings

Peel several large onions. Cut into thick slices and divide into rings. Dip these in milk, then in flour seasoned with salt and pepper. Cook in deep hot oil or fat for 3 minutes or so. Drain and serve.

Three recipes from Sheena Green Matthews's grandmother:

Green Tomato Chutney

5 pounds green tomatoes
½ pound onions, chopped
½ pound sugar
¼ pound sultana raisins
1 ounce dry mustard

1½ teaspoons curry
    powder
3 chilies
2 pints vinegar

Slice tomatoes and sprinkle with salt. Place in layers. Let stand for 12 hours. Drain. Put tomatoes and all other ingredients in a pan with the vinegar. Boil until thick and tender. Bottle in clean, hot, sterile jars.

Onion Dumplings

4 large whole Spanish onions	2½ ounces butter or shortening
6 ounces flour	4 ounces finely grated cheddar cheese
Pinch of salt, cayenne, pepper and baking powder	Cold water
	1 egg, beaten
	½ pint cheese sauce

Cook the onions in boiling salted water for approximately 1 hour or until tender. Drain and allow to cool slightly. Sieve the flour, salt, cayenne, pepper and baking powder and blend in the butter or shortening. Add the grated cheese and cold water to bind the mixture. Knead lightly and roll out to a rectangle 6 inches by 12 inches. Cut into 8 strips and brush each with the beaten egg. Place 2 strips criss-crossed over each of the onions, egg side down. Put on a greased baking sheet and bake in a moderately hot oven (375°) for 20-25 minutes. Serve hot with cheese sauce.

Pickled Onions

Take small unpeeled onions. Put in a basin and cover with brine made from 1 pound of salt to

one gallon of water or else sprinkle liberally with salt. Leave for 12 hours. Drain well or, if salted, rinse in cold water and then drain. Peel off the outer skins. Place in fresh brine for 24-36 hours. Wash in cold water. Drain well. Pack into jars with spiced vinegar, leaving room for at least ½ inch of vinegar on top of the onions. Seal the jars. Keep 3-4 months before using.

Spiced Vinegar

¼ ounce cinnamon bark	Several peppercorns
¼ ounce cloves	Pinch of cayenne
¼ ounce whole allspice and mace	1 quart white vinegar

Bring spices and vinegar to a boil in a covered saucepan (not brass, copper or iron) and let stand for two hours without further heating. Strain the vinegar. Use.

Shirley Singer's Salt Free Sauce

1 teaspoon oil	⅛ teaspoon crushed red pepper
2 or more cloves garlic, crushed or chopped	¼ teaspoon garlic powder (optional)

½ cup chopped onion
¾ cup chopped celery
  leaves
½ cup chopped green
  pepper
¼ cup chopped
  mushrooms
½ teaspoon oregano

¼ teaspoon onion
  powder (optional)
2 fresh ripe tomatoes
  or 4 plum tomatoes,
  skinned and chopped
  finely
2 12-ounce cans dietetic
  tomato juice

Put the oil in a skillet. Add everything except
the tomatoes and the juice. Saute until brown,
but not burnt. Then add the tomatoes and
juice. Stir and let simmer on medium heat for
1-2 hours until it thickens. Stir often.
Refrigerate what's left after use in tightly
covered jar. It will last for about two weeks.

Spaghetti Scalliano

1 pound spaghettini
  or thin linguine
Salt
4 tablespoons olive oil
Black pepper

6 or more tablespoons
  butter
8-10 thin scallions,
  cut into thin slices

Cook the pasta *al dente* in water to which salt
and 2 tablespoons of olive oil have been added.
Drain and return to the hot pot. Toss with the

pepper, the rest of the olive oil and the butter until the latter melts. Mix in the scallions. Toss. Sprinkle each serving with a few pieces of scallion. Serves 4.

Dave Ottiger's Fried Rice

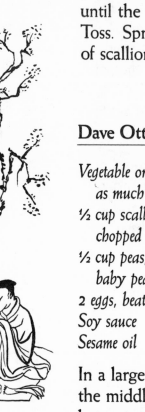

*Vegetable or peanut oil,
   as much as needed*
*½ cup scallions,
   chopped*
*½ cup peas, preferably
   baby peas*
2 eggs, beaten
Soy sauce
Sesame oil

*4 cups cold rice,
   preferably one day old*
*Whatever left over
   shrimp, chicken, beef,
   crab, vegetables you
   have (smoked sausage
   or chorizo is very
   good)*

In a large skillet or wok, put 3 dashes of oil in the middle. Saute the onions until translucent, but not over-cooked. Push them to one side. Add another dash of oil. Saute the peas lightly. Push to another side. Add more oil. Scramble the eggs in it. Push aside. Add more oil. Saute your other additions of meat, shellfish, fish or vegetables. Add a few drops of soy sauce and sesame oil. Add the rice. Stir until coated. Fry for 4-5 minutes. Reduce the heat and fold in the ingredients from the sides of the pan. Cook

another 5 minutes. Eat while crackling.
Serves 4.

Mickey's Spinach Salad

1 pound spinach   2-3 hard-boiled eggs
1 large red onion   1 can black olives

Wash and dry the spinach. Slice the onion and
the eggs. Mix all the ingredients together and
toss with the following dressing:

Dressing

¼ pint sour cream   Red wine vinegar
1 medium-sized onion,   Salt and pepper
  chopped

Blend the sour cream and the onion together in
a blender, food processor or a mortar until
smooth. Refrigerate for two hours. Add wine
vinegar, salt and pepper to taste. You may also
add any herbs you wish. Pour over the spinach.

And don't forget—onions on hamburgers, onions
on cheese sandwiches, onions in salads, onions
in stews. No wonder the annual per capita
consumption of onions in the U.S. is nearly 10
pounds!

GARLIC

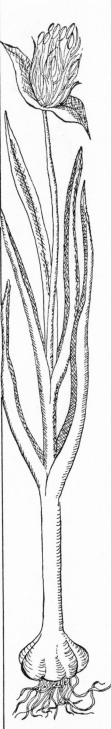

It is not really an exaggeration to say that peace and happiness begin, geographically, where garlic is used in cooking.

Marcel Boulestin

From the Chez Panisse Garlic Feast (printed in Garlic Times):
Whole Garlics and Mushrooms
(Champignons a l'ail aux feuilles de vignes)

Saute 15 whole mushrooms and 15 whole peeled garlic cloves in 1 cup of olive oil until slightly tender. Sprinkle with salt and pepper to taste, and a pinch of thyme and marjoram.

Lay a bed of grape leaves in a baking pan and place mushrooms and garlics on top. Lay another layer of grape leaves on top and drizzle with olive oil.

Bake for ½ hour at 350° or until mushrooms and garlics are very soft.

Serve warm in individual dishes, circling the mushrooms and garlics with the grape leaves. Serves 4.

Garlic Vinegar

Add several cloves of garlic to a bottle of white or wine vinegar. Let the garlic stay in the bottle as long as you like. The longer it stays—the stronger the flavor.

Tuna Risotto

3 tablespoons olive oil
4-6 cloves garlic
3 cups plum tomatoes

1 can tuna in
  olive oil
1 teaspoon basil

Fry the whole garlic cloves in the oil in a big skillet. Add the undrained tuna, tomatoes and basil. Cook until the liquid is reduced to a thick sauce. Serve on rice. Serves 4.

Pasta al Pesto

1 pound spaghetti
1 cup fresh basil leaves
⅓ cup pine or
  pistachio nuts
4 cloves garlic

¾ cup grated Parmesan
  or Romano cheese
½ cup olive oil
3 tablespoons butter

Cook the spaghetti *al dente*. While it is cooking, pound the basil, nuts and garlic in a mortar or blend in a blender or food processor. When

well mixed, add the cheese. Then, gradually add the olive oil and mix. Toss the spaghetti with butter. Pour the pesto sauce over it to taste. Serves 4.

Mock Boursin
(Devised by The Cheese Board in Berkeley, California)

1-2 or more cloves garlic, crushed	⅔ pound cream cheese
½ cup chives, minced	⅓ pound baker's cheese
½ cup parsley, minced	Salt to taste

Add the crushed garlic to the chives and parsley. Mix in with the cheeses and salt. Whip with an egg beater. Serve as a dip with vegetables, chips or crackers or as a side dish.

Hard-Boiled Eggs With Garlic Sauce

10 cloves garlic	Salt and pepper to taste
2 anchovies	6 hard-boiled eggs
1 teaspoon capers	2 tablespoons parsley,
4 tablespoons olive oil	chopped
1 teaspoon vinegar	

Put the peeled garlic cloves into boiling water and cook for 10 minutes. Drain and dry the garlic. Crush or pound in a mortar. Add the anchovies and capers and keep pounding until you have a smooth paste. You may also use a blender or a food processor. Gradually beat in the oil, a bit at a time. Add the vinegar and season with salt and pepper. Pour over the halved eggs. Sprinkle with parsley. Serves 4-6.

Bagna Cauda

2 cups heavy cream
4 tablespoons sweet
  butter
8 anchovies, finely
  chopped

1 tablespoon finely
  chopped garlic
1 small white truffle,
  finely chopped
  (optional)
⅛ teaspoon cayenne

Cook the cream over moderately high heat until it is reduced to 1 cup. In another pan, melt the butter (make sure it doesn't brown). Add the garlic and anchovies and cook briefly. Blend in the cream. Add the truffle and cayenne. Cook until hot, but not boiling. Serve with ice-cold scallions, peppers, carrots, cucumbers, broccoli, cauliflower, celery, mushrooms, etc., and Italian or French bread. Serves 6-8.

Queen Victoria's chef is said to have chewed garlic and breathed heavily over the salad to imbue it gently with a garlicky aroma. The Author feels a better way to imbue said salad is to rub garlic around the bowl or on a *chapon*— a dry piece of bread which is tossed into the salad. Better yet, why be a chicken? Try a garlicky salad dressing such as:

Shirley Singer's Salt-Free Salad Dressing

2 or more cloves
  garlic, crushed
1 tablespoon finely
  chopped onion
Pinch of garlic powder
  (optional)

Pinch of onion powder
  (optional)
2-3 lemons, juiced
1 ounce or so of oil
Pepper

Put the garlic, onion and powders into a cruet. Squeeze in the lemon juice. Blend in the oil. Shake well. Check that there's enough oil. Add pepper to taste. Shake again. Pour on the salad. Refrigerate after use. Before reusing, let stand at room temperature 15-20 minutes. Then, shake again and use.

The Best-Ever Sandwich

Alessio Balestra, owner of Villa Giulia in
Brooklyn, New York is one of the best chefs in
the world. And he told the Author the secret
recipe of his favorite sandwich, which she is
passing on to you lucky readers:

Fresh basil   *Olive oil*
Fresh garlic   *Bread*
Fresh plum tomatoes

Chop the basil and garlic; slice the tomatoes;
plop on the bread; drizzle on the olive oil;
mangia!

And remember—garlic rubbed on steaks,
chops, lamb, chicken, duck; garlic in egg
salad; garlic in tacos; garlic in tomato juice.
Herbalist Jeanne Rose advises tortillas with
garlic, avocado, yogurt or mayonnaise, alfalfa
sprouts or anything else you care to add.
Sounds good enough to eat.

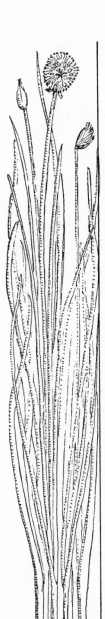

LEEK— "Poor Man's Asparagus"

Leeks can be used as a side dish or main course, plain or mixed with other vegetables. If you've never tried them, now's your chance. They're sweeter and milder than onions or garlic and also more nutritious.

German Leek Salad

8 leeks
½ cup sour cream
2 tablespoons lemon juice

1 teaspoon or more horseradish
Salt and pepper

Cook the leeks until tender. Drain. Chill. Mix the remaining ingredients and pour over the leeks. Serves 4 as a side dish.

Three Soups

Cock-a-Leekie

This is Scotland's national soup, immortalized by Sir Walter Scott in *The Fortunes of Nigel*—"Come my lords and lieges, let us all to dinner for the cock-a-leekie is a-cooling." Here is the recipe:

1 plump fowl and giblets *8 or more leeks, sliced*
1 bay leaf *2 tablespoons raw rice*
1 sprig parsley *1 dozen whole prunes*
Salt and pepper

Clean the fowl and giblets. Simmer in two quarts water with the bay leaf, parsley, salt and pepper and two leeks for 1 hour. Skim off the fat. Remove the fowl and giblets. Serve later as a course with the soup. Strain the soup. Add the other leeks, rice and prunes. Simmer 30 minutes or until the leeks are tender. Serves 6.

There are many variations on this soup. Onions, apricots, bacon, beef bones and various herbs may be added. Some omit the rice and prunes, but the latter is traditional.

Welsh Leek Soup

6 leeks *1 cup grated cheese*
4 tablespoons raw rice *(cheddar, Parmesan, etc.)*
2 cups milk *1 cup white wine*
Salt and pepper *Paprika*

Wash and chop the leeks into thin slices. Put them and the rice in a pot with enough water to cover. Simmer until the rice is done. Add the milk. Bring to a boil. Season with salt and pepper. Add the cheese and wine. Sprinkle paprika on each serving. Serves 4.

Vichyssoise
(Cold *Potage Parmentier*, attributed to Louis Diat)

4 cups coarsely chopped,
  peeled potatoes
3 cups leeks, thinly
  sliced
2 quarts chicken or
  vegetable stock or
  bouillon

1 teaspoon salt
Pepper
½ cup heavy cream
3 tablespoons chives,
  finely chopped

In a large, partially covered pot, simmer the potatoes, leeks, stock and salt for 40-50 minutes or until the vegetables are tender. Blend the mixture at a low speed in a blender or food processor, or force through a sieve into a bowl. Pour back into the pot. Season with salt and pepper and stir in the cream. Simmer until heated through. Sprinkle the chives on top. Serves 6-8.

CHIVES—
"Little Brother of the Onion"

Chives are super in salads, with sour cream on baked potatoes, mixed in butter (garlic and shallot butters are also terrific), in omelets, soups and virtually all cheeses. You may even pickle the small bulbs in vinegar. Or you can try:

A Dip to End All Dips

2 pints sour cream
3 tablespoons horseradish
2 tablespoons paprika
2 tablespoons chives, finely chopped
1 teaspoon salt

2 teaspoons dry tarragon or 3-4 teaspoons fresh tarragon
3 or more cloves garlic, crushed
¼ teaspoon pepper

Mix all the ingredients. Chill thoroughly (it's best if made the day before). Serve with vegetables and chips.

Chive-y Spread

½ pound cottage or pot cheese
1 cup chopped chives
8 radishes, chopped

2 pickles or gherkins, chopped
2 tablespoons sour cream
Salt and pepper

Mix all the ingredients together. Serve with black or rye bread. Serves 4.

You may also blend chives with parsley, garlic, salt and pepper into cream cheese. Chi-

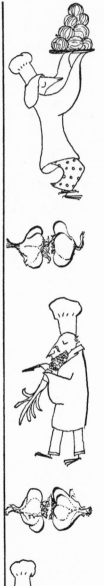

nese chives (*A. tuberosum*), also known as garlic chives, are delicious raw in salads or stir fried.

SHALLOTS

Many recipes say that you may substitute green onions for shallots. This is true—if you can't get shallots. But the Author advises you to try, because *nothing* else tastes quite like shallots—sweet, mild, piquant. You can subscribe to a monthly supply by mail from:

GNL Shallot Distributors
51 DeShibe Terrace
Vineland, N.J. 08360
Write for a price list.

Or you can grow them yourself—it's quite easy, as you'll see in the next chapter. Meanwhile, get them *somehow* and make:

Asparagus Vinaigrette

1 pound asparagus
1 ½ teaspoons wine
  vinegar
1 ½ teaspoons prepared
  mustard (Dijon is best)
Salt and pepper

¼ cup olive or
  vegetable oil
1 ½ teaspoons shallots,
  finely chopped
1 ½ teaspoons parsley,
  finely chopped

Break off the tough asparagus bottoms. Then peel the asparagus to remove the scales and top layer of skin. Steam or blanch until tender, but not mushy. While they are cooking, whisk the vinegar, mustard, salt and pepper together. Gradually add the oil, stirring constantly. Add the shallots. Drain the asparagus. Spoon over the sauce. Sprinkle on the parsley. Serves 4.

Beurre Blanc

¼ cup wine vinegar, preferably white

2 tablespoons lemon juice

2 tablespoons white wine or dry white vermouth

½ teaspoons salt

1-2 tablespoons finely minced shallots

⅛ teaspoon white pepper

2-3 sticks chilled butter cut into small pieces

Boil all the ingredients except the butter until reduced to 1½ tablespoons. Remove the pan from the heat and beat in two pieces of butter with a whisk. As the butter softens and creams, beat in another piece. Set the pan over low heat and, beating constantly, add the other pieces of butter, bit by bit, until the sauce is a thick, ivory-colored cream. Season to taste. Makes 1–1½ cups.

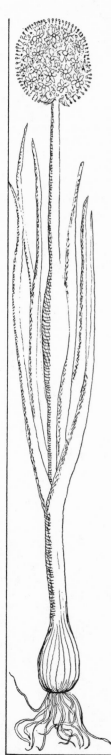

Shallots can be chopped and thrown into an infinite variety of dishes. They can also be pickled or roasted whole like garlic and small onions.

THE EGYPTIAN TOP ONION (Another edible onion)

Cook the stalks like leeks. Or chop into salads or other dishes. The small bulbils that form on the tops (hence the name) can also be eaten.

THE SELECTION, CARE AND HANDLING OF ALLIUMS

An English Superstition
You must buy onions only in a shop that has two doors.

BUYING ALLIUMS

Choose firm onions, garlic and shallots that are not discolored, sprouting or "pulling away" from the peels.

Generally, the larger the onion, the milder it is.

Choose leeks that are fresh and fine, with green parts unwilted.

Chives are hard to find—best to grow your own. If you *do* find them in a store, make sure they are fresh and unwilted.

STORING ALLIUMS

Store onions, garlic and shallots in a dry place, away from root crops and tubers such as potatoes. They rot more easily when exposed to such. You may also keep these alliums in the refrigerator, along with leeks. An added plus to this practice is that a cold onion makes you tear less.

It's not a good idea to keep halves of onions or garlic cloves around. Some people feel they collect contagions from the air. Whether or not that's true, they don't keep well and they tend to flavor other foods that are nearby like milk, cheese, fruit and chocolate. However, you can keep onion halves, well-wrapped or sealed, in the refrigerator. If you know you're going to need only part of an onion, don't peel it before cutting. It will keep better with the skin still on.

PEELING

You can drop onions and garlic briefly into boiling water and then drain; they will peel easily. Always peel from the root towards the top.

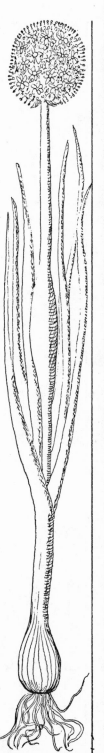

Pry cloves of garlic from the head with your fingernail.

You can also peel garlic easily by bringing the heel of your hand firmly down on a clove (don't smack it too hard if you don't wish to crush the clove). The flat of a knife will serve the same purpose as your hand, but will flatten the clove.

Onion peel is good in soup. Cook it and fish it out before serving—an easy task because it floats to the top.

The outer skins of scallions and leeks may also be peeled to clean them. Leeks tend to be sandy, so rinse them carefully.

And by the way—you can squeeze half an onion for the juice *with the skin on* like an orange.

A Texan Superstition
To keep from crying while peeling onions, put a little bit of onion skin on the top of your head.

Other A-Peeling Tales or How to Stop Crying While Skinning Alliums
1. Clamp bread, a match stick or a toothpick between your teeth.
2. Put a slice of bread on the end of the knife.
3. Refrigerate first or peel under cold, running water.

Note—The Author favors No. 3.

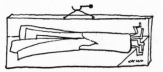

SLICING AND SUCH

A cut clove of garlic is stronger than a whole one.

A garlic press

is a good way to crush cloves—it yields the oils and "meat," while retaining the pulp. John Harris suggests pressing the cloves *unpeeled* to avoid the work of cleaning the press's tiny holes.

One clove pressed is approximately equivalent in strength to two to three cloves of similar size minced or chopped.

ODORS

To remove onion odor from your hands, sprinkle them with salt and cleanse thoroughly with soap and cold water. You can also rinse them under cold water, then rub with salt, chopped parsley, celery tops or lemon, and then wash with soap and cold water.

To remove the odor from knives and cutting boards, rub them with salt and water, lemon juice or a raw tomato.

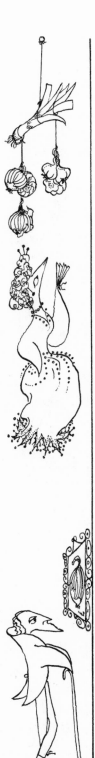

To kill cooking odors (if you care to do such a sacrilegious thing), set a cup of vinegar on the stove.

COOKING

Alliums brown quickly and burn easily. So, watch them carefully when sautéing, frying or the like. Follow recipe directions carefully to see if alliums should be translucent, golden or brown.

DRYING

Onions are suitable for drying. Slice into rings. Blanch for ½ minute. Then, spread on trays or racks in a warm, dry, well-ventilated place out of the sun. Turn occasionally, and let dry slowly. Store.

FREEZING

Most vegetables freeze well—leeks especially. Clean them. Blanch whole 3-4 minutes; sliced, 2 minutes. Plunge into cold water. Drain. Dry. Pack into freezer bags and freeze. They can keep for 6-9 months or longer.

Chives are also easy to freeze. Just pack into bags and pop in the freezer. Then you can have baked potatoes with sour cream and chives in the middle of winter.

DEHYDRATED AND POWDERED ONIONS AND GARLIC

Onions and garlic were successfully dehydrated for the first time on a commercial basis at the end of the nineteenth century. But it was not until the 1930's that dehydration was carried out on a large scale in Egypt, Eastern Europe and the U.S. Garlic and onion powder were basically World War I inventions. Today, dried onions and garlic are available *powdered, granulated, ground, minced, chopped, sliced* and in the form of *onion* or *garlic salt* (powdered onions or garlic mixed with ordinary table salt). Specially developed onions such as the Southport White Globe and the White Creole are grown for dehydration processing. California produces more than 70,000,000 pounds of dehydrated onions annually. Dried onion or garlic bits are reconstituted in about 30 minutes and may be used in place of fresh onions or garlic. Powder may be used for flavoring, as it is in lots of prepackaged foods. But, frankly, if you turn to these products, your Allium Consciousness is somewhat deficient. They *do not* have the flavorful taste of fresh alliums—nor do they have their healthful properties. The only dehydrated alliums the Author can contemplate the use of without wincing are dehydrated shallots or chives—and only because shallots and chives are often so darn

hard to find fresh. Otherwise, get out that red onion, that Mexican garlic, and use them the way the good Lord intended!

TO PREVENT ONION AFTERTASTE AND INDIGESTION

In *The New York Times*, Craig Claiborne suggests putting sliced or chopped onions in a sieve and pouring boiling water over them, then draining quickly under cold running water; or putting the onions in a bowl, pouring boiling water over them, draining immediately and adding cold water to cover and a few ice cubes to chill quickly.

TYPES OF ONIONS, TYPES OF GARLIC

There are so many kinds of cooking onions, it would be impossible to list all of them. But what we buy does fall into two general types—American onions, which are white, yellow or red, and small, dense, sharp, early ripeners and good keepers; and Foreign or European onions (which may be grown in America) like Spanish and Bermuda onions, which are larger, milder and more tender, but do not keep as well. Pick a type appropriate to your recipe—e.g., don't use sharp yellow onions in Grapefruit and Onion Salad; choose the mild Spanish or Bermuda onions instead. There are also many types of bunching onions or scallions. Some are *green onions*—or young *Allium cepa* plants—while others are *Welsh onions* ("Welsh" is a corruption of the German word *Walsch* or foreign), a distinct species—*Allium fistulosum*—or Japanese onions.

There are three major types of garlic:
Creole or American—*white-skinned, strongest.*
Italian or Mexican—*pink or purple outer skin.*
Tahitian—*also white and the largest.*

Garlic, like onions, is in season all year. C.F. Leyel also mentions a German red garlic which is hot with large clove clusters (four or five to the pound), but not as large as mild elephant garlic. But the Author has never seen it. She has, however, seen elephant garlic, which produces bulbs weighing one pound or more. These are extremely mild. In fact, some botanists have claimed that elephant garlic is *Allium scordoprasum* or *rocambole*, while the University of California's division of Agricultural Sciences claims that it is *Allium ampeloprasum*, a type of leek. Why the dispute? You'll find out in the next chapter. At any rate, elephant garlic is hard to find in a store. So, if you want some, grow it yourself. It can be ordered from a number of nurseries, but Nichols

178

Garden Nursery in Oregon claims to have originated it. Write for their pamphlet "The Story of Elephant Garlic" and their catalogue: Nichols Garden Nursery, 1190 No. Pacific Hwy., Albany, Oregon 97321.

Recently, *The New York Times* reported that Toshio Nakagawa has developed a strain of garlic that tastes like garlic, but doesn't leave the lingering odor on your breath. Will wonders never cease! There are also various varieties of leek (including a Mediterranean relative called *kurrat*), but not of chives or shallots. Why so many types of cooking alliums? Well, hybridizers are constantly trying to find types that are better for different dishes; types that grow better in cold places with short growing seasons such as Maine, or ones that do well in hot places with long growing seasons like Arizona; types that are milder or more pungent; types that resist disease better, etc. Somebody worked to develop those bulbs you chuck into your food. Somebody had to grow them, too. That somebody could be you.

Read on and you'll find out how.

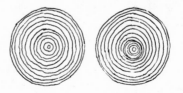

5.

ALLIUM BOTANY
AND
CULTIVATION

Los mejores ajos se siembran con malidiciones.
(The best garlic is sowed with curses.)
Andalusian proverb

Chives bring forth many leaves about a
hand-full high, long, slender, round like to little
rushes amongst which grow up small and tender
stalkes, sending forth certaine knops with
floures like those of the onion, but much lesser.
They have many little bulbes or headed roots
fastened together: out of which grow down into
the earth a great number of little strings, and it
hath both the smell and taste of the onion and
leeke, as if it were participating of both.
John Gerarde, The Herball, 1597

Gerarde's excellent description of *Allium schoenoprasum* shows how well naturalists from the Golden Age of Herbalism observed plants and their relationships to similar species. There are many such excellent descriptions and observations throughout the history of herbalism—from ancient Chinese texts to contemporary works. However, it was not until the 18th Century that a codified system of classification which showed plant relationships was invented by Linnaeus. He grouped plants by *Class, Order, Genus, Species* and *Variety*. Although this system has since been expanded to include *Phylum* or *Division* (a group of classes) and *Family* (a group of genera), it still holds. But taxonomists (people involved with plant or animal classification) have found that new sets of evidence often crop up to suggest changes in classification. And the order *Liliales* is particularly taxonomically difficult. Hence:

Hey, dilly, dilly,
They thought you were a Lily
'Cause they misclimbed your
botanical tree.
But don't resort to Valiums¹
You botanists, for Alliums
Are in the Amaryllis family.

1 Valium—a trade name for a tranquilizer.

Taxonomy's confusing.
And your patience may be oozing.
But, dear reader, please don't worry
*   and take heart.*
For you'll see how all the dozens
Of allium-y cousins
Relate, if you'll just follow
*   this nice chart.*

The Onion

Division
Old name: *Angiospermae*
New name: *Magnoliophyta*

Sub-Division
Old name: *Monocotyledonae*
    (commonly, the Monocots)
New name: *Liliatae*

Class
Liliopsida
Order
Liliales

Family
Amaryllidaceae

Genus and Species
Allium cepa

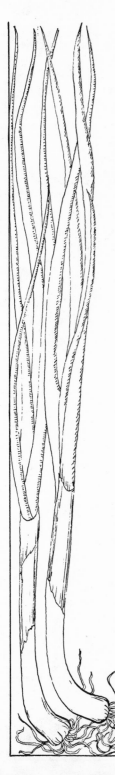

Some older taxonomists list:

Division
Spermatophyta

Class
Angiospermae

Sub-Class
Monocots

Order
Liliales

Family
Liliaceae or Amaryllidaceae

Genus and Species
Allium cepa

The Author will refer to the newer system.

What does this classification mean? Let's start with the largest grouping—the *Division*. *Angiosperms* are flowering plants that produce seeds enclosed within the pistil or mega-sporophyll (female reproductive organ) which later develops into a seed-bearing fruit. The new name for Angiospermae—*Magnoliophyta*—was created in an effort to create groups with names of plants that show the characteristics of the group they are in. In other words, magnolias are good

examples of flowering plants that produce seeds enclosed within the pistil, etc. So, they give their name to the classification. Onions (and the other alliums) are also such flowering plants, so they belong to this division.

There are two sub-divisions of the Division *Magnoliophyta*—Dicots, now called *Magnoliatae*, and Monocots or *Liliatae*. The *cotyledon* is the leaf-like structure enclosed within the seed, and it is responsible for the nourishment of the germinating embryonic plant. When you plant a seed and it sprouts, these are often the first leaves to appear. Dicots have two cotyledons; monocots have one. Monocots, now called *Liliatae* because lilies are good examples of them, are also distinguished by long narrow leaves with parallel veins which grow from the base, as well as other characteristics. If you watch an allium as it grows, you'll see the long spear-like leaves and other monocot characteristics.

Class, order and family are all categories defined by multiple correlations of character such as the position and number of reproductive organs (pistils and stamens); the type of flower (number of petals, sepals, symmetry, etc.); the leaf type; and other characteristics. The lily is much like the amaryllis and vice versa. And it's over their families that there's been so much recent dispute.

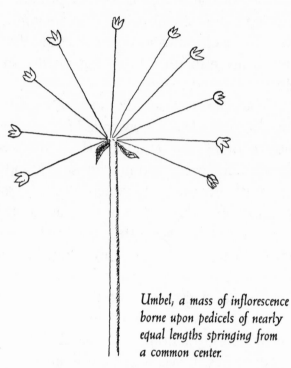

Umbel, a mass of inflorescence borne upon pedicels of nearly equal lengths springing from a common center.

Alliums have been classified both as part of the lily family and the amaryllis family. An allium resembles a lily in that in each, the ovary is free and superior (above the other organs and flower parts). It resembles an amaryllis in that its *inflorescence* (flower cluster) is *umbellate*—distinguished by a naked stalk terminating in one or more flowers borne from a common point (lilies have inflorescences that take other forms such as *racemes* and *panicles,* in which flowers are borne along an axis)—and surrounded by a *spathe* or sheath. In *Hortus III,* alliums are classified as members of part of the amaryllis family. But the dispute apparently still rages on. Thomas Delendick of the Brooklyn Botanic Garden says that Arthur Cronquist in *The Origin and Classification of Flowering Plants* recognizes the Amaryllidaceae as an artificial group not truly distinguished from the Liliaceae. So, he combines the amaryllids with the lilies under the latter name. But Armen Takhtajan (*Flowering Plants; Origin and Dispersal*) splits the Liliaceae into natural families, with the amaryllids one of these. However, he does not classify alliums among the amaryllids! He elevates them to Family Status: Alliaceae.

The remaining categories of plant classification—genus and species—also involve the position and number of reproductive organs, flower and leaf type, etc.—only the distinctions are now even finer. As stated at the beginning of this book, all of the 500 or so alliums are characterized by that famous smell and taste. They are also characterized by these distinctions:

1. The foliage leaves are usually basal (attached to an underground stem).
2. All segments of the *perianth* (the petals and sepals) are petal-like and free from one another to below the middle.

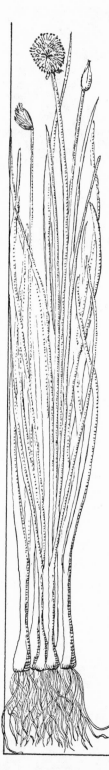

3. There are always six anther-bearing stamens in each flower (anthers are the pollen-bearing parts of the stamen).
4. The ovary is free and superior.
5. The umbellate inflorescence is surrounded by a single spathe.

According to allium expert Henry Jones, there are seven major *species* of edible alliums classified by bulb, leaf type, etc.:

1. *Allium cepa*—common onion
   Allium cepa aggregatum—multiplier or potato onions, shallots
   Allium cepa proliferum—top, tree, Egyptian onions
2. *Allium sativum*—garlic
3. *Allium ampeloprasum*—leeks, kurrats, rocambole
4. *Allium fistulosum*—Welsh, bunching onions
5. *Allium schoenoprasum*—chives
6. *Allium tuberosum*—Chinese or garlic chives
7. *Allium chinense*—rakkyo or ch'iao t'ou

Which allium is a variety of which species is constantly a matter of disagreement. For example, until recently, shallots were thought to be a distinct species (*A. ascalonicum*), but are now considered a type of "multiplier onion," *A. cepa aggregatum*. Japanese bunching onions were once grouped with Welsh onions—*A. fistulosum*—but they too are now classed as a variety of *A. cepa*. And leeks once listed as *A. porrum* are now thought to be a variety known only in cultivation of *A. ampeloprasum*, the wild leek. Thus—*A. ampeloprasum Porrum*. As you are reading this, taxonomists might be reclassifying all sorts of alliums.

It is not easy to classify a plant. That's why the argument mentioned in the previous chapter over what on earth elephant garlic is has not been so quickly solved. It has been called *A. scordoprasum* because, like rocambole, it is mild and purple-skinned and has a large bulb made up of big cloves, but like the leek, *A. ampeloprasum*, it has broad, flat leaves, folded lengthwise. Maybe in the next decade, we'll know the answer!

Onions are true bulbs consisting of a mass of fleshy leaves, called *scales*, folded over each other and filled with enough food to nourish the blossoms and leaves through the blooming period. That's why they don't even need soil to sprout. In the onion, the scales are thin and wrapped tightly around the bud. The covering of dry, papery leaves we call onion skin is the *tunic*. At the bottom, a disk of hardened stem tissue called a *basal plate* holds the scales together. It is from there that the roots emerge when the bulb is planted or placed in water. Onions—and leeks—

are *biennials*. This means they grow and store food in the bulb the first year and they flower the second year, after which the life of the plant is over. Welsh onions, on the other hand, like garlic and shallots, are *perennials*, coming back year after year as long as a portion of the plant is allowed to remain in the ground. Onions have hollow leaves and a flowering stem. The inflorescence is a globe-shaped head of white blossoms.

By contrast, garlic has a divided bulb. A new plant can grow from each clove, just as a new one can grow from each onion or leek seed. Garlic leaves are flat, as opposed to the onion's hollow ones. Garlic is a perennial—it comes back each year to flower and produce aerial bulblets. The flower stalk is approximately eighteen inches high, bearing a pink or purplish umbel. The shallot (and other aggregate and proliferate onions) produces bulblets, each of which will produce a plant. The leek is a bulbless plant with a thick white lower stalk and a green upper one with flat, ribbon-like leaves. The two to three foot high flower stalk bears a white, purple-marked umbel. But only leeks grown for seed are allowed to flower.

Like garlic, chives are perennials. But like leeks, they are bulbless and, like onions, they have hollow leaves. The foot high flower stalks bear lovely, lavender umbels.

Now that you know something about their botany, you are probably itching to grow them. So ... on to:

ALLIUM CULTIVATION

All alliums have the same basic requirements for developing into healthy—and tasty—plants:

1. Lots of sunshine. Onions will grow leaves in the spring and early summer, but will not bulb until the day length begins to shorten. There are short day onions which will bulb when daylight is twelve to thirteen hours long, and long day types which need up to sixteen hours of daylight. The former are usually grown in the South in winter or very early spring; the latter are the summer varieties grown in the North.

2. Space. Alliums are shallow-rooted and compact, so they tend to suffer from weeds and other competition. Six to twelve inches between plants is advised, depending on the allium.

3. Water. Give plenty, but do not flood or the bulbs will rot or mature late. Root growth is stimulated by water, not temperature or daylight. Good drainage is essential.

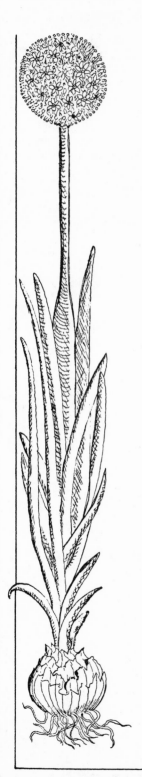

4. Ideally—deep, fertile soil of medium acidity, although too much nitrogen is not good. As alliums need high potassium, it is good to fertilize them with wood ash. Alliums and other plants also need calcium to neutralize high soil acid. Test your soil pH and, if needed, add bone meal, lime or some other calcium source. Bone meal (as well as rock phosphate, colloidal phosphate and granite dust) also supplies phosphorus, a mineral that has been called the "master key" to agriculture. Nitrogen is provided by animal manures, vegetable residues, meat, fish and blood meal and a variety of mulches. And good compost adds all sorts of helpful nutrients.

So, before you plant your alliums, pull any weeds and break up the soil. Turn into it your compost and fertilizers, rake smooth, dig your furrow or trench and plant. Remember, however, that alliums are among the least fussy of all vegetables; so, even if your soil is not perfect, they should grow for you.

5. Mulch. Not a necessity, but a darn good idea. Mulch is a layer of material

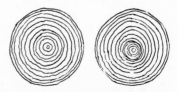

that is put on top of the soil to keep in moisture, keep out weeds, and ultimately improve soil structure and fertility. Use buckwheat hulls, hay, cocoa bean hulls, wood chips, pine needles, even paper disguised with grass clippings, as mulch. You'll be glad you did!

Those are the generals—now for the specifics.

ONIONS

Pick up a plant catalogue—*Burpee's, Park Seed* or whatever—and turn to the page(s) on onions. Did you know there were so many kinds to choose from? For years, plant explorers and hybridizers have been trying to improve onion varieties. For example, a plant explorer went to Iran in the early 20th Century and found in Kashan a small, tight-necked onion that helped California growers breed an onion resistant to *thrips*, a harmful insect. Plant breeders use baby houseflies to pollinate onion flowers. Buds from pollen sterile flowers are enclosed in bags with heads bearing the desired pollen. The flies are placed in the bag and as they move about, they transfer pollen from one parent to the other when

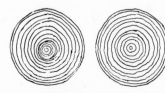

the buds open. Interesting, but, of course, this does not help you choose the hybrid for you. How do you choose? First, you read the descriptions. Then, you select the variety(ies) appropriate to your locale, your use and your taste. An example from the *Park Seed* catalogue:

Spartan Sleeper Hybrid 110 days.
High globular yellow with firm, tangy white flesh. Very productive, stores well. A good northern variety.

This description tells you that this variety, called *Spartan Sleeper Hybrid*, takes one-hundred ten days to develop into a bulb ready for harvesting. It is a yellow-skinned onion with sharp-tasting white meat. It grows and *stores* well (an important factor if you're planning on growing a lot of them to feed yourself and friends throughout the winter). And it is good for northern latitudes.

In catalogues, you will also come across mild red, sharp red, mild yellow, mild white, sharp white, sweet Spanish and other varieties, as well as ones which keep well and ones which don't. Take your pick—and make sure it is a good one for your area.

Onions may be grown from the 3 S's:
Seeds
Seedlings
Sets

There are advantages and disadvantages to each.

Seeds

It takes longest to get ripe onions from seed. Seeds are also more difficult to handle than seedlings or sets. But there are more varieties of onion seeds available than of seedlings or sets. They are also cheaper. You will have a better chance of success with seeds if you sow them indoors in flats (egg cartons will do) and transplant them when the ground is workable. To plant in flats, simply fill the carton or whatever with a growing medium (usually a prepackaged mix of peat, perlite, etc.), sprinkle on the seeds thinly and cover them lightly with the growing medium. Water and close the lid. Put in a warm place. When the seeds sprout and push against the lid, open it and put the carton in a sunny window. When the seedlings are several inches tall, thin them so they'll have room to grow. When they're four inches or so, and the soil is workable, you may plant them outdoors. To harden them off (get them used to the cold), leave the flat outdoors for longer and longer periods for several days. Seeds can also be grown in a cold frame or hot bed. Or, if you have patience, sow them directly in the ground one-half inch deep in rows one foot apart. Check seed

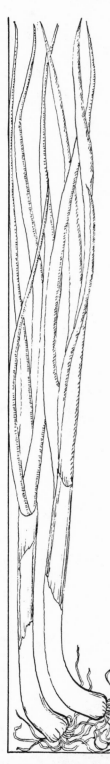

packets for further instructions. Scallions do well grown from seed in window boxes which are at least six inches deep. Welsh onions may also be grown from seeds or seedlings.

Note: Onions are hardy and can stand frost, so they may be planted in very early spring.

Seedlings

These are young onion plants grown from seeds in greenhouses or the like. They're a good way to get large Spanish and Bermuda onions. They handle fairly easily and they provide an earlier crop and larger onions than seeds. However, they are often harder to find than seeds or sets; they come in few varieties; they are more expensive than seeds or sets. And, as shown above, it's not so hard to grow your own seedlings, rather than buying them. However, if you don't have sunny windows or indoor space, purchased seedlings may be the answer. Set them in your garden three inches apart and thin from July on so that they eventually stand six or more inches apart. You may also plant them in bunches (six or so to a bunch) and let them develop after a few weeks into scallions rather than bulbs.

Sets

These are small, dry, immature onions which have been crowded so they haven't been able to develop fully. When they are planted once again,

they resume growth and become scallions in 6-8 weeks, bulbs in about 14 weeks. They are very easy to handle, produce bulbs sooner than seed or seedlings and do not require extensive seedbed preparation. But, like seedlings, they do not come in many varieties and they cost more than seeds. Choose small sets in which the bulbs are less than one-half inch in diameter—big bulbs are more likely to run to seed rather than bulb. Plant one to two inches deep (two inches if you want long, white necks), three to four inches apart (no wider or you will get split bulbs) in rows one foot apart. Make sure to plant them right side up— look for a little neck, often with a sprout.

Note: Planting and harvesting times vary across the country and throughout the world. Note time zones on seed packets and in catalogues.

FOUR ONION PLANTING MYTHS
(which may or may not be true)

Brazil
Gardeners believe that onions will not grow if they are not planted on Good Friday.

Georgia
Plant onions in the (moon) sign of the Reins (Libra), so they will attain full weight.

If onions are planted over potatoes, the latter won't suffer for moisture, as the onions will get in the potatoes' eyes and supply enough water for both vegetables.

Arkansas
Plant onions and potatoes far away from each other or the onions will "make a 'tater cry its eyes out."

TO GET ONION SEEDS
Use solid, well-ripened onions. Plant in a sunny, protected location, 6 or more inches apart. Apply compost mulch. When the plant flowers, stake the blossom. The seeds ripen slowly and the whole flower head must be dried under cover since they fall out easily. Package and use next year. Remember, though, onion seeds are comparatively short-lived and are usually not good after one or two years.

HARVESTING ONIONS
'Onions will rot if dug in the sign of the heart.'
Whatever that means, it sounds like interesting advice. Actually, in the North, onions are usually harvested in late August and September when Virgo (the sign of the guts) and not Leo (the sign of the heart) is in power. So the advice is probably sage.

Onions should be pulled up when the

foliage yellows and falls over. Be sure to withhold
water once this yellowing starts. Spread the bulbs
in the sun and let them dry for a few days to a
week. If it has rained, dry thoroughly in boxes
under cover. Then cut off the tops an inch above
the bulbs unless you wish to braid them. Store in
net bags in a cool, dry, dark place.

TO BRAID ONIONS
Cut one yard of twine. Tie a loop to act as a
hanger. Starting at the loop, braid the long dry
onion leaves into the two strands of cord, placing
the onions upside down on the braid. The
smaller onions should go at the top. There will be
about two dozen to each cluster. Knot securely at
the bottom. Hang in a clean, dry, cool place.
> *Note: Don't braid Spanish onions; they're too
> heavy and will break off.*

GARLIC

Garlic cloves may be ordered from nurseries or
bought in the supermarket. It doesn't much
matter—one is as good as the other, although the
garlic ordered from a nursery may be fresher.
There are no garlic seeds. Garlic is very easy to
grow. In loamy, slightly acidic soil (pH 6.5 or
thereabouts) with good drainage, place whole
unpeeled cloves, pointed side up, one to two

inches deep, four to six inches apart (further for larger heads; elephant garlic should be planted eight to ten inches apart in rows eighteen to twenty inches apart). Water regularly, keep weed free and watch your garlic grow. You may also plant cloves in containers indoors and out (provided you give them lots of sun) to grow garlic greens—delicious in salads and such.

Garlic may be planted in winter or very early spring (depending on the climate or locale) or the fall. Harvest in late summer or late fall when the tops yellow and droop as in onions. Pinch off early flowers to allow the bulbs to develop. Or you may allow them to winter in the ground. The second year, the bulbs will send up a flower which you may let bloom. It will also, if allowed, grow aerial bulblets which can be planted. Garlic may be braided like onions and hung in the shade to dry.

Garlic and the Moon
(two myths which may or may not be true)

The Romans suggested planting garlic when the moon was below the horizon and gathering it when the moon was nearest the earth to banish its strong aroma.

Dr. Fernie wrote:

As an instance of lunar influences (which

undoubtedly affect our bodily welfare), it is remarkable that if Garlic is planted when the moon is in the full, the bulb will be round like an onion, instead of being composed, as it usually is, of several distinct cloves.

LEEKS

Leeks are started from seed in the same way onions are. Because they take so long to grow (five to six months), they should be started in flats or cold frames. Plants should be spaced three inches apart, preferably in furrows or trenches, and thinned to stand six inches apart when the seedlings are as thick as a pencil. Eat the thinnings! When transplanting, cut the foliage halfway back to compensate for root damage. To produce high quality plants, *blanch* (whiten) the lower part by drawing up the soil or mulch in a mound around it to exclude light. Fertilize well with compost. Mulch to retain moisture. Harvest in the fall by lifting with a garden fork when the plants look fat enough. You may also leave them in the ground through the winter if you bank them halfway with soil and mulch the tops heavily. Leeks can be dug up in 20° weather—and the stalks thaw out perfectly. Or they can be harvested in spring as a super-early vegetable.

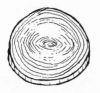

To Get Leek Seeds

Bank and mulch the parent leeks to protect from constant freezing and thawing. They should stand one and one-half feet apart from other plants in all directions. Support the blossom stem. The seeds mature fully only in warm summers and may then be gathered from the dry flower heads. Clip these and shake into bags. Like onion seed, ripe leek seed is coal black. Leeks cross easily with pearl onions, so avoid growing the two together.

SHALLOTS AND TOP ONIONS

Plant the bulbs or cloves as you would garlic—two inches deep, two to three inches apart. Like garlic, if started in the fall, plants mature in nine months. When planted in the spring, the clusters mature in three or four months, but are smaller. The greens may be cut and used like chives.

Top onions are grown from the top bulbils which give the plant its name. Cultivate as you would shallots.

CHIVES

They can be started from seed sown in pots or directly in the ground and covered with one-fourth to one-half inch of soil. They will then take a year to produce harvestable leaves. Don't thin the seedlings the first year. The following spring, transplant small groups of them five to six inches apart, leaving six or more plants in a group.

Or you can buy potted plants and set these in containers or in the garden, six inches apart. Chives are very hardy and a must for any herb garden. They also grow well in pots indoors in a sunny window. If potted chives are to be brought indoors for the winter, let them first freeze outdoors in their pots. Then, bring them in.

If allowed to produce their lovely lavender flowers, chives will seed themselves easily. If you do not want seeds, snip the flower heads as they fade to prevent seed formation. This will also encourage the plant to put its energy into growing more leaves. Chives are also propagated by division when the clumps become over-large.

How to Propagate Chives by Division

In early spring, carefully remove the clump of chives from the ground with a spading fork or trowel. Shake the soil from the roots. Separate them gently with your fingers, trying to break as few roots as possible. Pull the clump gently apart. You now have two clumps. Plant these at their previous growing level six inches apart, or give one away to a friend.

To Harvest Chives

To prevent weakening, cut whole spears from the outer edges of the clump, snipping off just above ground level. This practice is also better for the looks of the plant. Chives send up new leaves till midsummer, so don't be afraid to snip them frequently for cooking and such. Thalassa Cruso suggests that when the supply of new shoots diminishes, you should cut the chives to the ground, water heavily and fertilize, and you will see a new spurt of growth. Chives freeze well and may be packed into freezer bags for winter-time use.

OTHER EDIBLE ALLIUMS

Rocambole—*A. scordoprasum*, Serpent Garlic, Sand Leek, Rock Leek

> This plant has a curious bulbil-bearing stem that twists into a loop on its way up. It is propagated like top onions from these bulbils or like garlic from the underground bulb. The bulbils can be eaten like garlic, but without peeling.

Chinese Chives—*A. tuberosum*, Gow Choy

> Instead of a single bulb, one to three tubers develop on a horizontal rootstock. The leaves are flat, instead of cylindrical and

hollow. Plant as you would chives. Use fresh or lightly stir-fried. The buds may also be eaten in salads, with eggs, etc.

Potato or Multiplier Onion—*A. cepa aggregatum*
This has large, irregularly shaped bulbs with coppery yellow skin. It produces no seeds and is propagated by the lateral bulbs it freely produces earlier than ordinary onions. Plant in early spring (mid-winter in warm climates) almost on the ground surface, six to ten inches apart, in rows fifteen inches apart. If left in the ground to reach full maturity, each bulb will produce seven to eight bulbs of various sizes. However, you may harvest them in midsummer to late fall, depending on when they were planted.

THE ASTROLOGICAL ALLIUM

Many people believe in lunar and planetary planting. In this approach, which seems to work, the moon is divided into quarters as such:
New to half—1st quarter
Half to full—2nd quarter
Full to dark of the moon—3rd quarter
Dark to new—4th quarter.

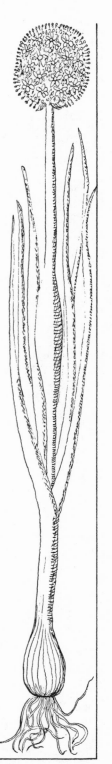

The full moon is the time of greatest growth, the new moon the least.

In general, because onions, leeks and garlic cloves have a medium-length germination time (eight to ten days), they are planted near the full moon to take advantage of the strong pull and increased light of the moon, whereas the more rapidly sprouting sets are planted near the new moon to enjoy the increased growth energies and activity as the the cycle progresses to the full moon.

Transplanting should be done near or right after the full moon, as the waning lunar gravita-

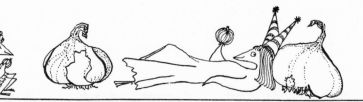

tional pull and light will stimulate root growth. Almanacs have good lunar planting calendars and suggestions.

Astrological planter Louise Riotte recommends planting garlic in the moon's first or second quarter under Scorpio or Sagittarius, and harvesting it in a fire sign—Aries, Leo or Sagittarius. Leeks should be planted in the second or third quarter under Sagittarius, and blanched in Gemini. Like garlic, onion seeds should be planted in the second quarter in Scorpio or Sagittarius, but sets should be set in the third or fourth quarter in Libra, Taurus or Pisces. Harvest all in a dry sign.

DREADED DISEASES AND CREEPY-CRAWLIES

Alliums are not prone to many diseases or bugs.[1] Moreover, they are known to repel harmful insects and other fauna. As poisonous chemical sprays often kill helpful insects and other animals (maybe even you!), to get rid of the few insects that pester onions and leeks, the Author recommends an organic approach.

---

[1] Many bugs—perhaps most—are *not* harmful. They may even be very helpful. Get out of the habit of squashing every bug you see.

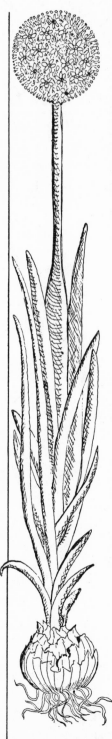

Onion Thrips

This nasty sucking insect may be controlled with *rotenone*, an organic insecticide from certain tropical plants, or, better yet, try *garlic*. Plant it among the onions or make a solution (see p. 209) to spray on the onions. Or, if your area is infested with thrips, plant Spanish onions which don't get them!

Onion Maggots

Maggots are rare in small gardens. If you get them, you need more organic matter—humus and potash and such—in your soil. You may also sprinkle tobacco around each plant or grow garlic or radishes near the onions. The first repels them; the second traps them. Hot pepper spray (cayenne or chilies in water with a little soap or detergent) is a good control. Or you can plant the onions in irregular rows so the maggot cannot find them easily—a technique that offers increased protection to other plants because many pests can't stand onion odor. You can also encourage *rove beetles* to inhabit your garden—they eat maggots. Or grow red or yellow onions; white ones are more prone to maggots.

Onion Fungi and Such

Onions (and leeks) can be attacked by smut, downy mildew, pink root and neck rot. Smut and

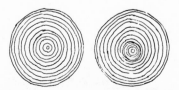

mildew can be avoided by using sets, rather than seedlings, or by spraying with *horsetail grass* solution, and by providing good air circulation. Pink root is thwarted by good fertilization and weed control, as well as control of the maggot fly which can cause wounds that leave the plant open to this disease. Neck rot means a storage problem; cure the bulbs well before storing in an airy container.

COMPANION PLANTING
or
What say, Let's be Buddies!

Certain plants like each other. And when they do, they may keep nasty bugs from each other, encourage better pollination, increased yields, better taste and odor, etc. No one knows exactly *why* certain plants make good companions—or especially why certain plants keep pests away. There are theories that strong-scented herbs mask the odor of their companions so bugs can't find them or that bugs don't like the strong odor or that repellent herbs give off root exudations that build up in the soil and destroy the eggs or larvae of pests or that they have aerosols that "bomb" bad bugs. At any rate, the alliums Love and are Beloved by many plants.

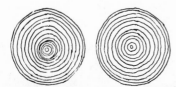

Garlic

Prone to *no* pests, this Good Buddy repels all sorts of them. It chases carrot fly, aphids, Japanese beetles, peach leaf borer (and leaf curl), green fly, weevils, mosquitos, maggots, bean beetles, etc.—the list goes on and on. Garlic is also supposed to shoo skunks, rats and snakes and, as William Cole wrote in *Cole's Art of Simpling,* "...if the garden is infected with moles, garlic will convince them to leap out of the ground presently." Garlic is also said to make raspberries grow better and roses smell sweeter. Maybe the roses are competing with the garlic! In fact, garlic may be planted near almost anything to improve it—except for beans and peas, the growth of which garlic and other alliums seem to inhibit.

Onions

They like beets, broccoli, carrots and cabbages. They repel carrot flies and cabbage worms. And chamomile, lettuce and summer savory like onions—that is, they help onions grow better. Again, don't plant them near beans and peas.

Leeks

Celery or celeriac and leeks do well in alternate rows. Leeks and carrots help the growth of one another and, like the other alliums, leeks repel carrot fly. No beans and peas near leeks, please.

Chives

Plant chives near roses to keep off aphids, carrots to shoo carrot flies, and apple trees to prevent apple scab. Try as a border around a celery patch. Keep away from beans and peas.

ALLIUM INSECTICIDES AND FUNGICIDES

Why spritz deadly chemicals on your plants, when you can spray *Alliums*—harmless to beneficial bugs, birds and you, but death to crummy crawlers and feisty fungi. Recent research has shown that *garlic* repels or kills an amazing number of insects including mosquitos which carry yellow fever and encephalitis and other plant pests that growers swore could only be zonked by lethal DDT. Other research indicates that garlic is not only *not* harmful to other animals, but actually helps surrounding wildlife (e.g., Rabbits show more resistance to *myxomatosis*, a killer disease among them). David Greenstock of The Henry Doubleday Research Association in England has come up with the following insecticide; it can be used against a variety of pests:

Soak 3 oz. of good chopped garlic in 2 tsp. of mineral oil for 24 hours. Slowly add a pint of water in which ¼ oz. of oil-based soap has been dissolved. Stir well. Strain and store

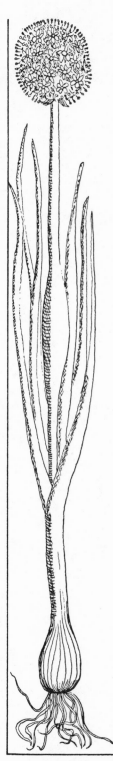

the liquid in a glass or china container so that it doesn't react with metals. Dilute 1 part to 20 parts water to begin with, then 1 to 100 thereafter. Spray.

The Author uses crushed garlic in water on her roses and watches the aphids drop off. Shallot or chive spray is also good against aphids. Onion spray is excellent for mites. Chive spray combats apple scab and downy and powdery mildew on gooseberries and cucumbers. Garlic, onion or chive spray can control potato and tomato blight and the brown rot of stone fruits. All of these sprays are simply the chopped herbs infused and diluted in water—one part to three parts water, then more water to dilute. Try them and you'll grin as the aphids fall off your roses, too!

TWO COMPANION PLANT DISHES

Frenchified Zucchini

1 pound zucchini, thinly sliced	1 tablespoon shallots, finely chopped
2 tablespoons butter	1 tablespoon parsley, finely chopped
Salt and pepper to taste	

Melt the butter in a frying pan. Add the sliced zucchini. Stir. Sprinkle with the salt, pepper

and shallots. Cook about 5 minutes or until the zucchini is tender, but not mushy, and lightly browned. Sprinkle with parsley. Serves 4.

Super Salad

Take a few bunches of greens (4-5 cups)—*lettuce, romaine, endive, dandelion, spinach, watercress, what have you.* Mix with ½ cup *chopped parsley* and 1 tablespoon each of fresh chopped: *Marjoram, Tarragon, Basil, Thyme, Salad burnet, Chives,* or any other herbs you care to use. This salad is best if the herbs are *fresh.* If you use dried herbs, use only *one teaspoon* each.

Mix in a bowl and toss with this dressing:

½ cup olive or vegetable oil	*1 teaspoon chopped onion*
¼ cup wine or herb vinegar	*¼ cup catsup*
1½ tablespoons sugar	*½ teaspoon Worcestershire sauce*
⅓ teaspoon salt	*1-2 cloves crushed or chopped garlic*

Serves 4.

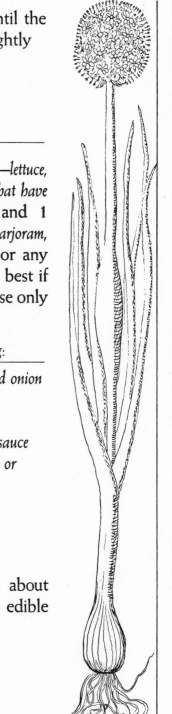

You should now know something about how edible alliums grow, how to grow edible alliums, and how to use edible alliums to let other plants grow.

But there are other alliums you may not want to eat and wild ones you may not want to grow. They can be interesting companions too, as you're about to see.

6.

OTHER ALLIUMS

Holy Moly!

The bushes in the woods and hedgerows are spanned over and twisted upon by the woody cords of the honeysuckle: the cloves of leaf these bear are some purple, some grave green. But the young green of the briars is gay and neat and smooth as if cut in ivory. One bay or hollow of Hodder Wood is curled all over with bright green garlic.
Gerard Manley Hopkins, *Journal*, 1871

Swamp Onion. Sierra Garlic. Shortstyle Onion. Siberian Chive. Nodding Wild Onion. Crow Garlic. Bear's Garlic. Little Prairie Onion. Ramson. Golden Garlic.

In the beginning of April, woods all over the temperate regions of the world are garlic-, onion-

and leek-covered, for there are many wild alliums springing to life in the early spring. Some of them—like Hopkins's *A. ursinum* (most likely)—are greeted with fondness by naturalists, and with joy by hungry backpackers. Others, such as *A. vineale* or Crow Garlic, are listed by the U.S. Agricultural Service as obnoxious weeds. But at least everyone agrees that they have pretty names—as you can judge from the above. Let's meet a few of these wildlings.

Allium vineale

The "garlic that grows in vineyards," Crow Garlic, Field Garlic, Onion Grass

In city parks and gardens, by roadsides, in country fields, this is the wild garlic you will most often see, its long chive-like leaves growing one to two feet high and smelling very oniony indeed. It got the name Crow Garlic from the belief that if crows eat it, they will be stupefied. Farmers detest this garlic because it is very stubborn and prolific and can interfere with other crops. Dairy farmers especially hate it because cows like to munch it and produce garlic-flavored milk. However, *A. vineale* has been used as a potherb. And on spring days, it is pleasant to pluck the leaves and nibble them—as long as you don't mind the resulting odor on your breath.

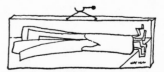

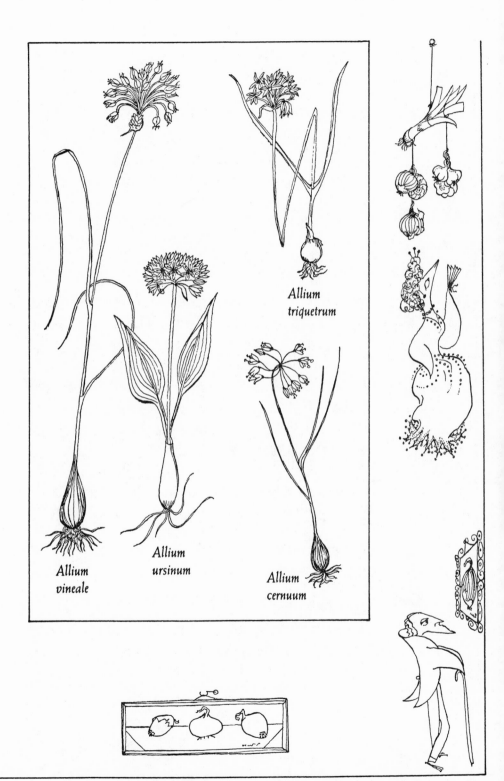

Allium
triquetrum

Allium
cernuum

Allium
ursinum

Allium
vineale

Allium ursinum

Ramson, Broad-leaved Garlic, Bear's Garlic

This allium has broad leaves similar to those of the Lily-of-the Valley and white, star-like flowers. It likes semi-shade and grows six to sixteen inches in woods and ravines. The name *ramson* comes from the "ram" or male sheep, alluding to its strong smell.

Allium triquetrum

This wild leek has similar cultivation tastes to *A. ursinum*. It has a three-leaved eighteen inch stem which supports umbels of white green-striped flowers that look rather like Star of Bethlehem (*Ornithogalum umbellatum*). One of the most interesting facts about both *A. ursinum* and *A. triquetrum* is that they are dispersed by *ants!* How? The stems become limp and lie flat on the ground. Then the *arils* (seed coats) of the seeds become impregnated with an oil that is delectable to the ants who carry the seeds about until they finally settle down to eat the arils and leave the seeds ready to germinate.

Allium tricoccum

Wild Leek, Wild Onion, Ramp

Sweet and flavorful, this is the allium glorified and eaten at the Ramp Festivals (see p. 14). It too inhabits woodlands and slopes. Its white flowers are borne on bare stalks in June or July. Its broad leaves appear from April to June and wither before the flowers appear.

Allium cernuum
Wild Onion, Nodding Onion, Little Prairie Onion, Lady's Leek

A pretty eighteen inch wildling that grows in full sun. The leaves are slender like chives. The pendulous flowers are subtly scented umbels of white, pink or purple. They bloom in June and July. The bulbs are tasty and may be dug from May to August. The Tewa and the Hopi nations called it the "little prairie onion" and ate it raw in salted water with corn dumplings or pieces of *piki bread* (made of blue cornmeal) or roasted it in ashes and dried it for winter use.

A WORD ON WILD ALLIUMS

If you want to pick and eat them, make sure of two important things:
1. That where you are it is legal to pick them.
2. That what you are picking is really an allium. *All* alliums have the distinctive onion odor when crushed or bruised. The bulbs especially have a strong smell. If the smell is missing, DO NOT EAT. What you have could be

Fly Poison or Death Camass (or even Lily-of-the-Valley), which are deadly— or at least capable of making you very, very sick. In fact, it is best to go wild herb gathering with an experienced wild herb gatherer, so that everyone returns home safe and sound and sated.

ALLIUMS IN THE GARDEN

Their beauty is such as to win admittance . . . notwithstanding the unnegotiable evils of their savour.

Reginald Farrer, *The English Rock Garden*, 1919

By now, you should know that the English are not fond of the allium odor. However, in her article "The Ornamental Onion," Pamela Harper points out that Farrer was an early ornamental allium supporter, who recognized that alliums have uses aside from the culinary and medicinal.

Ornamental alliums range from six inches to five or more feet tall. Their color range is wide— there are blue, purple, pink, red, white, cream, yellow and greenish umbellate allium flowers. They usually have the same growth requirements as edible alliums. As for odor, many of them have a lovely fragrance and smell oniony only when touched or bruised. Here are some popular garden alliums:

Allium moly—Allium luteum

The Great Moly of Homer, Serpent's Moly, Withering Moly, Sorcerer's Garlick, Lily Leek, Golden Garlic, The Inchaunter's Root

Sweet is the rose, but grows upon the brere/And sweet is moly, but his root is ill.

Edmund Spenser

The legendary plant does smell sweet, but quite oniony if you tread on it or cut it. It is a small plant (nine to twelve inches) with yellow flowers that multiplies rapidly, needs to be divided every few years, and makes a good ground cover. It is one of the few alliums that needs semi-shade. A popular plant, it is available through numerous nurseries both in bulb and seed form.

Allium neopolitanum

White Allium, Cascade Bells, White Stars

Six to twelve inches and the darling of many a garden and florist shop. It is a tender bulb, not reliably hardy north of Maryland. The flowers are white, pristine-looking, sweet-smelling, appearing in June. They are often used in bridal bouquets. *A. neopolitanum* is a good bulb for *forcing*—refrigerating or freezing for several or more weeks, then planting in a pot indoors so that it blooms out of season.

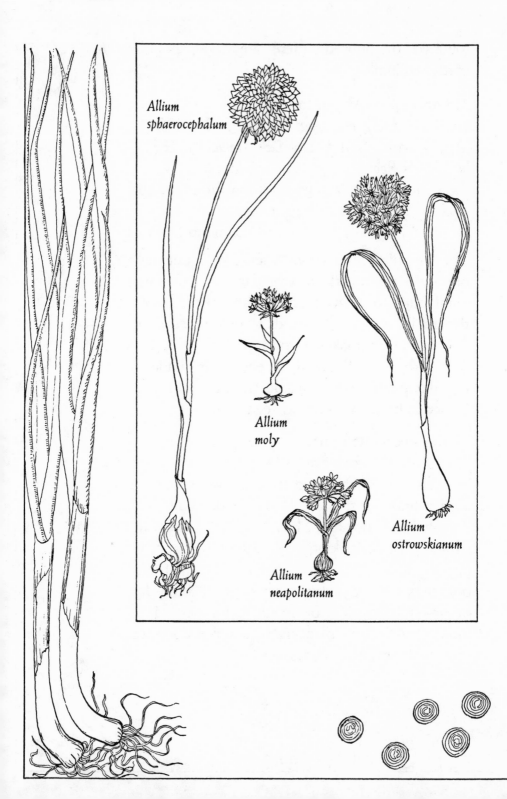

Allium sphaerocephalum

Allium moly

Allium ostrowskianum

Allium neapolitanum

Allium ostrowskianum—A. oreophilum
Rose Stars, Rosy Bells

The Author has a flock of these in her garden and highly recommends them. They are very easy to grow and available from many nurseries. The plants are six to eight inches high with pink, starry flowers that bloom in late spring or early summer. Good for rock gardens.

Allium giganteum
Goliath Allium, Globe Allium

A. giganteum lives up to its name. The plants are four to five feet high with large, globular purple flower heads that bloom in May and June. As they are stiff and formal, they look best in a small group rather than singly. And they are beautiful in dry arrangements. They are also expensive but worth it. Two related, shorter species are *A. aflatunese* and *A. rosenbachianum*.

Allium sphaerocephalum
Drumstick Allium

This is another of the Author's favorites. *A. sphaerocephalum* grows two to three feet high and produces wonderful purplish-crimson tight-headed flowers that resemble drumsticks (what you beat, not eat) in early summer. The bulbs are cheap and very hardy.

Allium senescens glaucum

Six inches with lavender pink, late summer or early fall-blooming flowers. The leaves are stunning—gray-green, curving like scimitars. The whole plant looks like a Japanese flower arrangement. It is best bought as a pot grown specimen and then planted outdoors.

Allium caeruleum—A. azureum

Azure Allium, Azure Skies

Known and loved for its two inch globular bright blue flowers which appear in June. The plant is eighteen inches to three feet tall and sometimes produces little bulbils among the flowers which may be planted.

Allium christophii—A. albo-pilosum

Star of Persia

Pamela Harper's favorite ornamental allium. An ethereal looking, two inch high plant with large, starry, light purple flower heads that have a metallic sheen. They bloom in May or June and are perfect for drying. The leaves die down after the flowers appear.

There are innumerable other alliums, but it would take another book to describe them all. And anyway, a picture *is* worth a thousand words. So pick up a catalogue—or, better yet, go to your nearest botanic garden and ask to see the alliums. You'll be surprised—pleasantly.

7.

FUN WITH ALLIUMS

There's more to an allium than meets the nose.

The first chapter of this book indicated some of the many historical uses of alliums—from summoning a deity to forecasting the weather. These uses may or may not be fantastical. The following uses are guaranteed to be wholly practical and/or artistic.

INVISIBLE INK

To write Letters of Secrets: . . . You may. . . write with vinegar or the juice of limon or onion: if you would read the same, hold it before the fire.

For those of you who have never made invisible ink, here's a translation of the above: Squeeze an onion into a glass or plastic container.

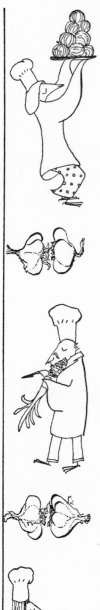

Dip a clean brush into the juice. Write your message on white paper. To read it, hold it up to a light.

PRINTING WITH ONIONS

Like other vegetables, onions can be used for block printing. Cut an onion in half. Stick a nail or long needle through each half to hold the layers together. Then, put each on paper towels or cloths to let the moisture drain. When the onion halves are dry, brush tempera paint or printing ink on each. On clean paper (with a padding of paper towels, cloths, etc., underneath to act as a blotter), press down the onion. Lift carefully to avoid smudging. Make a few test prints before attempting the "big one." You can also print fabric this way.

DYEING WITH ONIONS

Baked Eggs

Jack Passalaqua, owner of Bellamellio in Brooklyn, New York, showed the Author an old Sephardic recipe. Take a batch of eggs and boil them in a big pot with a pile of onion skins for five to fifteen hours. The eggs become a russet brown both outside and inside. They taste nutty and distinctively un-eggy. Jack uses them in macaroni salad and his customers swear they're eating ham!

Onion skins make a great Easter egg dye, too. Boil a quart of skins for at least 5 minutes. Strain. Cool. Dip in hard-boiled eggs. The longer the eggs sit in the dye, the brighter (or deeper) the color, ranging from pale yellow or tan to brass-red. Red or yellow skins may be used.

Besides dyeing eggs, onion skins can also be used to dye cotton or wool or other fabrics. Everyone has a favorite dyeing recipe. Here's a general one:

2 quarts of onion peels will make 2 quarts of dye.

Onion dye tends to fade, so a *mordant* must be used on the cloth or fabric to make the dye permanent. Different mordants create different colors. John Lust says that alum as a mordant on wool creates a burnt orange color: chrome on wool makes a brass color: and copperas and blue vitriol on wool make green when onion skins are used. For onion dye, a good mordant is:

2 *tablespoons alum*
1 *teaspoon cream of tartar*   *Per Gallon of Water*

Therefore, if you use a 2 gallon pot, you will need to *double* the above measurements. Use only enamel or stainless steel pots (aluminum

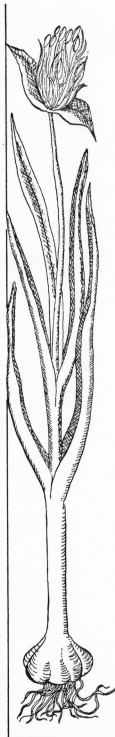

and other metals can mess up the dye) and wooden or steel spoons for stirring.

To Treat with a Mordant

Take a 2 to 4 gallon pot. Fill with water almost to the top. Add the alum (which you can get at a pharmacy) and the cream of tartar (which you can get at a grocery store). Set on the stove and simmer.

Wet the fabric and put into the pot to soak. Let it simmer for one hour.

Dyeing

While the fabric is soaking and simmering in the mordant, put the onion peels in another 2 to 4 gallon pot. Add enough water to cover. Simmer for 1 hour. Strain.

Then, the fabric should be soaked and the dye ready at the same time. Take the material out of the mordant. Wring slightly and put into the dye. *Simmer* (don't boil) for 1 hour. Stir frequently.

Rinse the material and spread it out in a warm, dry place, out of the sun. You may leave it for a week to let the dye set. If the dye is still strong, it may be kept for a short time in a closed container in a cool place. This dye is a particularly lovely one for wool or cotton tee-shirts.

Another Use of Alliums in the Arts

Sculptors rub garlic on weak spots in Carrara marble to harden them.

Onions and Microscopes

Peel an onion. Separate the layers carefully. You will find a sticky, membranous, almost transparent skin. Put it on a slide. Look at it under a microscope. You will see a good example of plant cell composition.

Hints for Carefree Motoring

A windshield rubbed with sliced onion will stay clear on rainy days.

Alliums and the Home

In Portugal the juice of the onion is used in lamps with the commoner sorts of oil, as it is supposed to have the effect of causing it to burn with a clear light.

G. Merle, *The Domestic Dictionary and Housekeeper's Manual*, 1842

To brighten the gold leaf of picture frames, rub them with boiled onion juice, then wipe dry.

To take spots or stains out of linen:

Take the juice of lemon and red onion mixed together, put to it a little salt and heat it gently over a fire, and then dip the part that is stained often in it: let it then dry, and get in readiness a hot lather of soap and water, to wash it immediately; and doing so in two or three washings it will quite disappear.

Royal Society of Arts, *The School of Arts*, 1754

Dr. Fernie says that as garlic is mucilaginous, garlic juice can be used as a glue for broken glass or china. Unfortunately, he does not say how to use it. If you know, tell the Author.

To restore color to scorched linen:

½ pt. of vinegar, 2 oz. of fuller's earth, 1 oz. of dried fowls' dung, ½ oz. of soap, the juice of 2 large onions. Boil all these ingredients together to the consistency of paste; spread the composition thickly over the damaged part, and if the threads be not actually consumed, after it has been allowed to dry on, and the place has subsequently been washed once or twice, every trace of scorching will disappear.

Mrs. Beeton, *Beeton's Book of Household Management*, 1861

Decorating with Alliums

At Succoth (Succos), the Jewish Feast of Booths—a harvest festival held in early fall—Jews decorate the *succah* with fruits and vegetables. If you have a succah, why not hang red onions, green and white leeks and white garlic bulbs among the other edibles? Alliums are excellent for succah decoration because they do not spoil quickly—a boon as they must hang there for a week.

If you have a tree at Christmas, do what the

Brooklyn Botanic Garden does—hang fruits and vegetables from it. After all, the Christmas tree is taken from an ancient pagan fertility and resurrection symbol, so symbols of the earth's fertility are appropriate decorations. Red onions look especially pretty.

Dried allium flowers or seed pods are beautiful in flower arrangements, wreaths, etc. You can wait until they dry on the plant and snip them, or dry indoors by hanging them upside down in a dark, cool place.

Use alliums to make figures as centerpieces or for prizes or party favors. Katherine N. Cutler in *From Petals to Pinecones* suggests creating a clown made from an eggplant (body), an onion (head), a carrot (hat), with a cauliflower floret necklace, a red pepper mouth, bean arms and eyes and nose made of cloves. You can use alliums in all sorts of ways in all sorts of figures.

An Allium Toy
The Chippewa made whistles from the stems of wild onions (*A. stellatum*). They let the stems dry a bit, cut a sound hole in the side and blew across the end.

And now for a different end—the end of this book. The Author hopes you have found it

both funny and informative. And if you didn't, maybe you should read it again.

To leave this chapter and this book on a jolly note, let us all have a sing-along and chime out the following to the tune of "My Favorite Things":

My Allium Things

Garlic near roses,
And chives in my salad,
Onions on burgers
That never taste pallid,
Vichyssoise dishes—a treat fit for kings,
These are a few of my allium things.

Shallots in sauces,
And leeks on the table,
Bright golden moly
of story and fable,
Allium ursinum blooming in springs,
These are a few of my allium things.

When my head aches,
When my nose runs,
When the world is bleak,
I simply surround me with allium things—the
    garlic, the onion, the leek!

MAY THE ALLIUMS BE WITH YOU!

Books for Suggested Reading

Bothwell, Jean, *The Onion Cookbook*, New York: Dover Publications, Inc., 1950.
Not just recipes—lots of material on onion lore and handling.

Conran, Terence and Maria Kroll, *The Vegetable Book*, New York: Crescent Books, 1976.
Cooking, lore, cultivation—all illustrated with beautiful, full-color pictures.

Crockett, James Underwood, Ogden Tanner and the Editors of Time-Life Books, *Herbs*, Alexandria, Va.: Time-Life Books, 1977.
An excellent, general book on herb gardening.

Friedlander, Barbara and Bob Cato, *The Great Garlic Cookbook*, New York: Macmillan, 1975.
Excellent recipes and odd facts about superstition, history and handling of garlic.

Grieve, Mrs. M., *A Modern Herbal*, 2 Vols., New York: Dover Publications, 1971.
One of the two best modern herbals I've come across.

Hall, Alan, *The Wild Food Trail Guide*, New York: Holt, Rinehart and Winston, 1973.
Wild alliums to gather and eat. What they look like, how to find them.

Harris, Lloyd J., *The Book of Garlic* (revised edition), San Francisco: Panjandrum/Aris Books, 1979.
Funny and packed with information. A garlichead's bible.

Hylton, William, ed., *The Rodale Herb Book*, Emmaus, Pa.: Rodale Press, 1974.
One of the most complete books on everything about herbs—with an organic approach.

Lovelock, Yann, *The Vegetable Book—An Unnatural History*, New York: St. Martin's Press, 1972.
Exotic information on a variety of vegetables.

Lust, John, *The Herb Book*, New York: Bantam Books, 1974.
My other favorite modern herbal.

Mendelsohn, Oscar A., *A Salute to Onions*, New York: Hawthorn Books, Inc., 1965.
A whimsical, personal book about onions with much information and recipes.

Mestel, Sherry, ed., *Earth Rites*, Vol. I, Brooklyn, N.Y.: Earth Rites Press, 1978.
Very clearly presented herbal remedies.

Morton, Julia, *Herbs and Spices*, New York: Golden Press, 1976.
A little "Golden" book with excellent illustrations of the edible domestic alliums—including Chinese chives and rocambole.

Rodale, Robert, ed., *The Basic Book of Organic Gardening*, New York: Organic Gardening/Ballantine Books, 1971.
The essentials of organic gardening—with information on leeks, onions, chives, garlic.

Scully, Virginia, *A Treasury of American Indian Herbs*, New York: Crown Publishers, 1970.
A dictionary written in a lively style on Native American uses of many plants, including garlic and onions.

Bibliography
BOOKS AND PAMPHLETS

Airola, Paavo, *The Miracle of Garlic*, Phoenix, Arizona: Health Plus, Publishers, 1978.

Angier, Bradford, *Field Guide to Edible Wild Plants*, Harrisburg, Pa.: Stackpole Books, 1974.

Beisly, Sidney, *Shakespeare's Garden*, London: Longman, Green: Longman, Roberts and Green, 1864.

Bold, Harold C., *The Plant Kingdom*, Englewood Cliffs, N.J.: Prentice-Hall, 1977.

Bothwell, Jean, *The Onion Cookbook*, New York: Dover Publications, Inc., 1950.

Brooklyn Botanic Garden, *Handbook on Herbs*, Brooklyn, N.Y.: Brooklyn Botanic Garden, 1958.

————*Herbs and Their Ornamental Uses*, Brooklyn, N.Y.: Brooklyn Botanic Garden, Spring, 1972.

————*The Home Vegetable Garden*, Brooklyn, N.Y.: Brooklyn Botanic Garden, 1972.

234

————*Japanese Herbs and Their Uses*, Brooklyn, N.Y.: Brooklyn Botanic Garden, 1968.

————*Natural Plant Dyeing*, Brooklyn, N.Y.: Brooklyn Botanic Garden, 1973.

Brothwell, Don and Patricia, *Food in Antiquity*, New York: Frederick A. Praeger, 1969.

Burtis, C. Edward, *Nature's Miracle Medicine Chest*, New York: Arco Publishing Co., 1971.

Camp, Wendell H., Victor R. Boswell, John R. Magness, *The World in Your Garden*, Washington, D.C.: National Geographic Society, 1957.

Chang, K.C., ed., *Food in Chinese Culture*, New Haven: Yale University Press, 1977.

Claiborne, Craig, *Cooking With Herbs & Spices*, New York: Harper & Row, 1970.

Clarke, Charlotte Bringle, *Edible and Useful Plants of California*, Berkeley, Ca.: University of California Press, 1977.

Clarkson, Rosetta E., *Herbs and Savory Seeds*, New York: Dover Publications, 1972.

Coats, Alice M., *Flowers and Their Histories*, New York: McGraw-Hill, 1956.

Conran, Terence and Maria Kroll, *The Vegetable Book*, New York: Crescent Books, 1976.

Cosman, Madeleine Pelner, *Fabulous Feasts—Medieval Cookery and Ceremony*, New York: George Braziller, 1976.

Crockett, James Underwood, *Crockett's Victory Garden*, Boston: Little, Brown and Co., 1977.

Crockett, James Underwood, Ogden Tanner and the Editors of Time-Life Books, *Herbs*, Alexandria, Va.: Time-Life Books, 1977.

Cross, John and Linda, *Kitchen Crafts*, New York: Macmillan, 1974.

Cruso, Thalassa, *Making Vegetables Grow*, New York: Alfred A. Knopf, 1975.

Cutler, Katherine N., *From Petals to Pinecones*, New York: Lothrop, Lee and Shepard, 1969. (Nature crafts.)

Dampney, Janet and Elizabeth Pomeroy, *All About Herbs*, Secaucus, N.J.: Chartwell Books, Inc., 1977.

Darby, William J., Paul Ghalioungui and Louis Grivetti, *Food: The Gift of Osiris*, London: Academic Press, 1977.

De Baïracli-Levy, Juliette, *The Complete Herbal Book for the Dog*, New York: Arco Publishing Co., 1977.

De Lys, Claudia, *Treasury of Superstitions*, New York: Philosophical Library, 1957.

Densmore, Frances, *How Indians Use Wild Plants for Food, Medicine and Crafts*, New York: Dover Publications, 1974.

Fernald, Merrit Lyndon and Alfred Charles Kinsey, *Wild Plants of Eastern North America*, New York: Harper & Row, 1958.

Fitzgibbon, Theodora, *A Taste of Wales*, London: Pan Books, Ltd., 1971.

Folkard, Richard, *Plant Lore, Legend and Lyrics*, London: Sampson Low, 1884.

Friedlander, Barbara and Bob Cato, *The Great Garlic Cookbook*, New York: Macmillan, 1975.

Garlic Times, Inaugural issue, 1977; #2, April, 1978; #3, Spring, 1979; #4, Summer, 1979; #5, Fall, 1979.

Gilbertie, Sal and Larry Sheehan, *Herb Gardening at Its Best*, New York: Atheneum, 1978.

Gordon, Lesley, *Green Magic*, New York: Viking Press, 1977.

Grieve, Mrs. M., *A Modern Herbal*, 2 Vols., New York: Dover Publications, 1971.

Griffith, F. L. and Herbert Thompson, eds., *The Leyden Papyrus—An Egyptian Magical Book*, New York: Dover Publications, 1974.

236

Hall, Alan, *The Wild Food Trail Guide,* New York: Holt, Rinehart and Winston, 1973.

Harris, Ben Charles, *Better Health With Culinary Herbs,* New York: Weathervane Books, 1971.

———— *Kitchen Medicines,* New York: Weathervane Books, 1968.

————*Make Use of Your Garden Plants,* Barre, Mass.: Barre Publishing, 1978.

Harris, James and Kent R. Weeks, *X-Raying the Pharoahs,* New York: Charles Scribner's Sons, 1973.

Harris, Lloyd J., *The Book of Garlic* (revised edition), San Francisco: Panjandrum/Aris Books, 1979.

Harrison, Molly, *The Kitchen in History,* New York: Charles Scribner's Sons, 1972.

Hatfield, Audrey Wynne, *Pleasures of Herbs,* New York: St. Martin's Press, 1965.

Health Research, *Garlic* (Revised Edition, 1977-78), Mokelumne Hill, Ca.: Health Research, 1978. (Large, unsifted compendium. Can be obtained through mail order.)

Hedrick, U.P., ed., *Sturtevant's Edible Plants of the World,* New York: Dover Publications, 1972.

Hehn, Victor, *The Wanderings of Plants and Animals,* London: Swan, Sonnenschein and Co., 1888.

Henisch, Bridget Ann, *Fast and Feast, Food in Medieval Society,* University Park, Pa.: The Pennsylvania State University Press, 1976.

Hill, Albert F., *Economic Botany,* New York: McGraw Hill, 1952.

Hottes, Alfred Carl, *Garden Facts and Fancies,* New York: Dodd, Mead and Co., 1949.

Howarth, Sheila, *Herbs With Everything,* New York: Holt, Rinehart and Winston, 1976.

Hylton, William, ed., *The Rodale Herb Book,* Emmaus, Pa.: Rodale Press, 1974.

Indiana Botanic Gardens. *The Herbalist Almanac*, Hammond, Indiana: Indiana Botanic Gardens, Inc., 1979, 1978, 1977, 1976, 1974, 1970, 1968, 1965, 1959.

Jobb, Jamie, *My Garden Companion*, San Francisco: Sierra Club Books/ Charles Scribner's Sons, 1977.

Jones, Henry A. and Louis K. Mann, *Onions and Their Allies*, New York: Interscience Publications, Inc., 1963.

Kato, Yoshio, *Garlic—The Unknown Miracle Worker*, Amagasaki, Japan: Oyama Garlic Lab., 1973.

Kaufman, William I., *The 'I Love Garlic' Cookbook*, Garden City, N.Y.: Doubleday and Co., 1967.

Kennett, Frances, *Folk Medicine, Fact and Fiction*, London: Marshall Cavendish, 1976.

Killion, Ronald G. and Charles T. Waller, *A Treasury of Georgia Folklore*, Atlanta: Cherokee Publishing Co., 1972.

Kordel, Lelord, *Natural Folk Remedies*, New York: G.P. Putnam's Sons, 1974.

Kraft, Ken and Pat, *Exotic Vegetables*, New York: Walker and Co., 1977.

Kramer, Samuel Noah, *History Begins at Sumer*, Garden City, N.Y.: Doubleday/Anchor Books, 1956.

Landry, Robert, *The Gentle Art of Flavoring*, London: Abelard-Schuman, 1970.

Lavine, Sigmund A., *Wonders of Herbs*, New York: Dodd, Mead and Co., 1976.

Law, Donald, *The Concise Herbal Encyclopedia*, New York: St. Martin's Press, 1973.

Leland, Charles Godfrey, *Gypsy Sorcery and Fortune-Telling*, New Hyde Park, N.Y.: University Books, 1962.

Leyel, C.F., *Compassionate Herbs*, London: Faber and Faber, Ltd., 1946.

———*The Magic of Herbs*, London: Jonathan Cape, 1926.

238

Lorwin, Madge, *Dining With William Shakespeare*, New York: Atheneum, 1976.

Lovelock, Yann, *The Vegetable Book—An Unnatural History*, New York: St. Martin's Press, 1972.

Lucas, Richard, *Common and Uncommon Uses of Herbs for Healthful Living*, West Nyack, N.Y.: Parker Publishing, 1969.

——*The Magic of Herbs in Daily Living*, West Nyack, N.Y.: Parker Publishing, 1978.

——*Nature's Medicines*, London: Neville Spearman, 1968.

Lust, John, *The Herb Book*, New York: Bantam Books, 1974.

Masefield, G.B., M. Wallis, S.G. Harrison and B.E. Nicholson, *The Oxford Book of Food Plants*, London: Oxford University Press, 1969.

McBride, L.R., *Practical Folk Medicine of Hawaii*, Hilo: The Petroglyph Press, 1975.

McDonald, Lucile, *Garden Sass—The Story of Vegetables*, New York: Thomas Nelson, Inc., 1971.

McPherson, Alan and Sue, *Wild Food Plants of Indiana and Adjacent States*, Bloomington: Indiana University Press, 1977.

Mendelsohn, Oscar A., *A Salute to Onions*, New York: Hawthorn Books, Inc., 1965.

Mercatante, Anthony S., *The Magic Garden*, New York: Harper & Row, 1976. (Plant lore.)

Mestel, Sherry, ed., *Earth Rites*, Vol. I, Brooklyn, N.Y.: Earth Rites Press, 1978. (Herbal remedies.)

Meyer, Clarence, ed., *American Folk Medicine*, New York: Thomas Y. Crowell Co., 1973.

Meyer, Robert, Jr., *Festivals U.S.A. & Canada*, New York: Ives Washburn, Inc., 1967.

Morrison, Sarah Lyddon, *The Modern Witch's Spellbook*, New York: David McKay and Co., 1971.

Morton, Julia F., *Folk Remedies of the Low Country*, Miami, Florida: E. A. Seemann Publishers, 1974.

————*Herbs and Spices*, New York: Golden Press, 1976.

Muir, Ada, *The Healing Herbs of the Zodiac*, St. Paul, Minn.: Llewellyn Publications, 1959.

New York Botanic Gardens, *Herbetia*, 1944-45, New York: New York Botanic Garden, 1945. (Garden yearbook.)

Nichols Garden Nursery. *The Story of Elephant Garlic*, Albany, Oregon: Nichols Garden Nursery, 1978 (?).

Niethammer, Carolyn, *American Indian Food and Lore*, New York: Macmillan, 1974.

Norman, Barbara, *Tales of the Table*, Englewood Cliffs, N.J.: Prentice-Hall, 1972.

Null, Gary and Steve Null, *Herbs for the Seventies*, New York: The Health Library/Robert Speller and Sons, Publishers, 1972.

Palos, Stephan, *The Chinese Art of Healing*, New York: Bantam Books, 1972.

Philbrick, Helen Louise and Richard B. Gregg, *Companion Plants & How to Use Them*, New York: Devin-Adair Co., 1966.

Quinn, Vernon, *Vegetables in the Garden*, Philadelphia: J.B. Lippincott Co., 1942.

Radford, E. and M.A., *Encyclopedia of Superstition*, London: Hutchinson & Co., 1961.

Randolph, Vance, *Ozark Magic and Folklore*, New York: Dover Publications, 1947.

Riotte, Louise, *Planetary Planting*, New York: Simon and Schuster, 1975.

Robbins, Ann Roe, *25 Vegetables Anyone Can Grow*, New York: Dover Publications, 1974.

Rodale, Robert, ed., *The Basic Book of Organic Gardening*, New York: Organic Gardening/Ballantine Books, 1971.

Roen, Rick and R. Kim Finley, *The Helix Herbal Album*, Boulder, Co.: RFM Publishing Corp., 1978.

Rose, Jeanne, *Herbs and Things*, New York: Grosset and Dunlap, 1972.

————*Kitchen Cosmetics*, San Francisco: Panjandrum/Aris Books, 1978.

Rosengarten, Frederic, Jr., *The Book of Spices*, New York: Pyramid Books, 1969.

Saggs, H.W.F., *The Greatness That Was Babylon*, New York: Mentor Books, 1972.

Sanecki, Kay, *The Complete Book of Herbs*, New York: Macmillan, 1974.

Saunders, Charles Francis, *Edible and Useful Wild Plants*, New York: Dover Publications, 1948.

Schaeffer, Elizabeth, *Dandelion, Pokeweed and Goosefoot*, Reading, Mass.: Young Scott, 1972. (Nature crafts for young people.)

Schafer, Violet, *Herbcraft*, San Francisco: Yerba Buena Press, 1971.

Scully, Virginia, *A Treasury of American Indian Herbs*, New York: Crown Publishing, 1970.

Simmons, Adelma Grenier, *Herb Gardening in Five Seasons*, New York: Hawthorn Books, 1964.

Skinner, Charles M., *Myths and Legends of Flowers, Trees, Fruits and Plants*, Philadelphia: J.B. Lippincott Co., 1911.

Sloane, Eric, *Folklore of American Weather*, New York: Duell, Sloan and Pearce, 1963.

Stobart, Tom, *Spices and Flavorings*, New York: McGraw-Hill, 1970.

Tannahill, Reay, *The Fine Art of Food*, South Brunswick, N.J.: A.S. Barnes and Co., 1968.

————*Food in History*, New York: Stein and Day, 1973.

Thesen, Karen, *Country Remedies*, New York: Harper Colophon Books, 1979.

Thiselton-Dyer, T.F., *The Folklore of Plants*, New York: D. Appleton and Co., 1894.

Thomson, William A. R., *Herbs That Heal*, New York: Charles Scribner's Sons, 1976.

Tribe, Ian, *The Plant Kingdom*, New York: Bantam Books, 1970.

Vogel, Virgil J., *American Indian Medicine*, New York: Ballantine Books, 1973.

Warner, Charles Dudley, *My Summer in a Garden*, Boston: James R. Osgood and Co., 1871.

Watanabe, Tadashi, *Garlic Therapy*, Tokyo: Japan Publications, Inc., 1974.

Wood, Magda Ironside, ed., *Herbs*, London: Marshall Cavendish, Ltd., 1976.

Zŏng, In-Sŏb, ed., *Folk Tales From Korea*, London: Routledge and Kegan Paul, 1952.

OLD HERBALS

(In Chronological Order)

Dioscorides, *De Materia Medica*, 1st or 2nd Century A.D. Reprint: 1938.

Pliny the Second, *Natural History*, 78 A.D.

John Gerarde, *The Herball or General History of Plants*, 1597.

Nicholas Culpeper, *The English Physician*, 1662.

John Evelyn, *Acetaria*, 1699. Reprint: Brooklyn Botanic Garden, 1937.

MAGAZINE AND NEWSPAPER ARTICLES

Baggett, James R., "Let Us Praise the Lowly Onion," *Horticulture*, April, 1977.

Claiborne, Craig, "Garlic—Folklore and Refined Tastes," *The New York Times*, April 23, 1979.

————"The Worldly Delights of Garlic," *The New York Times*, March 21, 1979.

Craig, Laura, "The Gardener's Kitchen: Garlic," *Horticulture*, September, 1979.

Derrenbacher, David, "Amaryllids," *Horticulture*, April, 1979.

Field, Michael, "All About Garlic," *Holiday*, June, 1966.

Harper, Pamela, "The Ornamental Onion," *Horticulture*, August, 1976.

Hills, Lawrence D., "Will Garlic Replace DDT?" *Organic Gardening and Farming*, September, 1972.

Kilborn, Jean, "The Overlooked Leek," *Horticulture*, April, 1976.

Langer, Richard W., "Planting Time for the Versatile Leek," *The New York Times*, March 1, 1979.

Levitt, Beverly, "Garlic, Fact and Fable," *Bestways*, October, 1974.

Maugh, Thomas H., "It's Nothing to Cry About," *Science*, April 20, 1979.

Roueché, Berton, "A Friend in Disguise," *The New Yorker*, October, 1974.

Strouse, Jean, "The World According to Garlic," *The New York Times Magazine*, December 9, 1979.

Wright, Betty Jane, "The Orange County Onion Harvest Festivals," *New York Folklore Quarterly*, Vol. II, August, 1976.

Index of Recipes

Index

260

  derivation of English word,
    52
  in history, 2, 53
  repelling pests with, 210
Sham-en-Nassim (Coptic Easter
    Monday), See festivals
Shao Hsin-Ch'en, 26
Shih Ching (The Book of Songs), 24
Siberia, 53
Sir-Sava (the Garlic Feast), See
    festivals
slicing alliums, 173
smell, causes of alliums,
    101-106
Smith, Rev. Sydney, 150-151
smut, See diseases and pests of
    alliums
Sokaris festivals, See festivals
Sourdain, Peter, 67
Spain and Spanish, 18, 64, 66,
    71-72, 77, 118, 148-149
species, botanical, 181-182,
    185-187
species of alliums,
  A. aflatunese, 221
  A. ampeloprasum, 177, 186-187
  A. ampeloprasum Porrum, 187
  A. ascalonicum, 2, 186
  A. caeruleum—A. azuerum, 222
  A. cepa, 177, 181-182, 186-187
  A. cepa aggregatum, 186, 203
  A. cepa proliferum, 186
  A. cernuum, 217
  A. chinense, 186

species of alliums (cont'd.)
  A. christophii—A. albo-pilosum,
    222
  A. fistulosum, 177, 186-187
  A. giganteum, 221
  A. haematochiton, 35
  A. moly—A. luteum, 40, 219
  A. neopolitanum, 219
  A. ostrowskianum—A. orephilum,
    221
  A. porrum, 187
  A. rosenbachianum, 221
  A. sativum, 71, 186
  A. schoenoprasum, 180, 186
  A. scordoprasum, 177, 187, 202
  A. senescens glaucum, 222
  A. sphaerocephalum, 221
  A. stellatum, 229
  A. tricoccum, 216-217
  A. triquetrum, 216
  A. tuberosum, 168, 186,
    202-203
  A. ursinum, 214, 216
  A. vineale, 214
spells, See charms, spells, and
    curses
Spenser, Edmund, 219
Stevenson, R.L., 75
Stoker, Bram, 60
Stoll, A., 105-106
Strouse, Jean, 123
sub-class, botanical, 182
  monocots, 182
sub-division, botanical, 181,
    183